March 2012

Dear Erin,
This little boo[k]
[t]o me & has brou[ght]
[v]ery dark times

[ex]perience periods in which we feel
[th]at God isn't listening, doesn't hear us,
[i]s ignoring us, is unreasonably making
[u]s wait for answers. None of those
[thi]ngs are true, of course.

In these pages I find an explanation
[of] God's silences that encourages me
[to] hold on. For me, the chapters 'In
[th]e Center Ring' has resonated deeply
[in] the past few months, but they
[al]l help.

You, darling daughter, the amazing
[cr]eation of God using some of our
[be]st & worst parts to form the wonder
[th]at is Erin Rebecca Woods, have had
[yo]ur seasons of 'silence' & waiting. Most
[like]ly, there will be more in your future.
[?] Jeannette wrote: "We live in a noisy
[wor]ld. Sometimes God has to be silent
[to] get us to hear them at all."
You are such a blessing to so many.
[?] thank God for you.

Much love,
Mom

troubling deaf heaven

troubling deaf heaven

Assurance in the Silence of God

jeannette clift george

BROADMAN
& HOLMAN
PUBLISHERS

NASHVILLE, TENNESSEE

Copyright © 2005 by Jeannette Clift George
All Rights Reserved.
Printed in the United States of America

10-digit ISBN: 0-8054-3191-8
13-digit ISBN: 978-0-8054-3191-9

Published by Broadman & Holman Publishers,
Nashville, Tennessee

Dewey Decimal Classification: 248.84
Subject Heading: SPIRITUAL LIFE \ CHRISTIAN
LIFE \ FAITH

Unless otherwise noted, all Scripture quotations are taken
from the Holman Christian Standard Bible®, Copyright,
© 1999, 2000, 2002, 2003 by Holman Bible Publishers.
Used by permission.

1 2 3 4 5 6 7 8   09 08 07 06 05

This book is dedicated to my friends who stand by me in
my times of need, stand for me in my times of ministry,
and sit with me at the table of celebration.

Acknowledgments

Thanks to Deborah Eckols for her professional attention to the compiling of this book and for her personal attention to my needs. Also a special thanks to Jan Simpson, my Intellectual Property attorney, who added the gracious touch of her friendship.

When, in disgrace with fortune and men's eyes,
I all alone beweep my outcast state
And trouble deaf heaven with my bootless cries
And look upon myself and curse my fate.

—From "Sonnet 29" by William Shakespeare

Table of Contents

Foreword		xiii
Chapter 1	Connecting the Disconnected	1
Chapter 2	Exits and Entrances	11
Chapter 3	The Flight of the Butterfly	27
Chapter 4	Help Wanted, Applause Needed	37
Chapter 5	A Well-Weathered Bookmark	47
Chapter 6	Tick Tock	53
Chapter 7	It's Your Cue	61
Chapter 8	Baggage Tags	73
Chapter 9	Well Done	81
Chapter 10	Survival in the Storm	89
Chapter 11	Sometimes When God Says Nothing, It May Mean Nothing	105
Chapter 12	Jacob Wasn't the Only One with a Lame Excuse	113
Chapter 13	Freedom in Need	123

Chapter 14   Whose Line Is It Anyway?   137

Chapter 15   In the Center Ring   145

Chapter 16   Surprise Celebration   159

Chapter 17   Home Address   171

Chapter 18   And the Winner Is . . .   179

Chapter 19   Some Ice Carvings Never Melt   183

Foreword

In writing this book, I refer frequently to the Great Book—the Bible. Most often it is referred to solemnly and accurately as the Word of God. I hear the echoes of its intoning pronouncement even as I write these words. I believe that solemnity, but my references are often gleeful. In that Book I found, and still find, joy.

Getting into the Word of God has never been an easy journey for me. I now teach Bible classes and am still a beginner in the Book. I am not a scholar or a theologian, nor can I open my Bible instantly to the Scripture I am seeking. I am frequently frustrated by my lack of scholarship and the fact that at one or two book-signing parties, I have signed beneath my signature a verse of Holy Writ which is not even in there because I got the chapter and verse numbers reversed! And then, I have given people Scriptures that will change their lives, and because I chose the wrong verse, the life-changing experience was real but not so positive as I had hoped. After the many years since my return to Jesus as Lord, I am still a novice in his Holy Workbook, but I find truths in its holy statements that fit my deepest needs and delight my highest hopes.

Initially, I fought its pages vigorously. Someone told me to read the Bible until I understood something from the reading. After an hour of intense reading (I think I had started with the Book of Leviticus) I threw my copy of the Bible across the room and cried aloud to God, "Yes, I have learned something! I have learned that I don't understand your Book! Now, can I stop reading it?" And then, still muttering over the details of my problem, I went over and picked up my Bible, with its tossed pages all askew, and read again. My early Bibles show the wear and tear of my struggle. Come to think of it, my current Bible does too. I admit it—I need a new Bible, but everything I know is in the margins of this one!

I kept reading. Not well organized. Not in a Bible class, which I highly recommend whether you are a beginner or not—maybe not Leviticus as a starter. Not with the wisdom of continuity—just reading, and reading, and weeping because I found nothing that made sense. And then, one day, one reading, all of a sudden I saw me in the Scripture. My need—my question for the day, my tears for the evening, my fears for the morning, me—in God's Holy Word. That made all the difference in the world. That's why I keep referring to Scripture. That's why I keep praying even when God's silence infers the communication is out of order. That's why I trust the reasons behind the teaching of God. Because I found me in his Word because he put me there. God put me in his Word that I might hear him in the silence, that I might hear him in the midst of my arguments with him, that I might know that he knows me and loves me because he said so. I share more of the details in a later chapter, but the Bible was not an open book until my heart was opened to it.

> When I lost myself in him, I found me.
> 1 Corinthians 15:10: "By God's grace I am what
>   I am,"
> and by his grace, even in the overwhelming he is
>   the undergirding.
> I am me because he promised.
>
> I am me in the cross fires of life's dilemmas—
> I am a realist, and real life is often out of sorts.
> I am a questioner and often out of answers.
> But I am still me because God said so.

That is why within this book you will find many references to the Great Book. You will also see a collection of memos. The reason they are there is because they didn't fit anywhere else. As I write, I keep two scratch pads handy to write down what I'm thinking about while I'm writing about something else. I do not recommend the process. It adds to clutter, is not administratively clear, and gives people the impression that I am not well organized. However, it works for me.

I have recently become a liberated woman and set myself free from the imprisonment of how-to books. I also encourage all writers, actors, and artists to disallow the presence of critics while you are writing, acting, or applying yourself to the practice of your art. Critics have a place, but it is not during the process. To me, the process itself is holy ground and is to be celebrated with great respect. God will surely get us from Monday to Monday, but he leads us through Tuesday, Wednesday, Thursday, Friday, Saturday, Sunday to get us there. If you skip any part of the process, you might lose a day, or worse, lose the purpose of the process which was that with which God blessed you in the first place.

You will find a few stories and poem-phrased thoughts and a few prayers that were actually prayed before they were written down. Some were answered positively and some were not. That is the freedom of God's sovereignty. Prayer is, in itself, a registered belief in God and his blessed sovereignty. If I thought I was in charge, I would not pray freely. In fact, if I thought I was sovereign, I would probably not pray at all.

In this book you will find references to people and matters intrinsic to my life that may have no meaning in yours. The following brief glossary may help you:

Lorraine Malcolm George—Husband. Yes, Lorraine. A truly wonderful man. A builder of massive things like freeways and overpasses and new patternings for old riverbeds, he took the time and attention to build a football field in an impoverished neighborhood and transformed a meeting hall into the theater in which I now work.

A.D. Players—A Christian theater company in Houston. I was working full-time in the acting company of Houston's Alley Theatre and was asked to teach an acting class at Houston Baptist College.

I agreed to do that but requested that I have no morning classes because I would be performing in the evenings. I also asked that I not teach freshmen because I felt acting should be taught later in the curriculum. So for two years I taught Freshmen Acting at 9:00 in the morning! From those students I began a small drama group that became an independent theater with extensive programming.

Residences—San Angelo, Texas; Houston, Texas; New York City; and back to Houston.

Education—Stephens College, University of Texas, various acting classes, and the intensive workshop of today.

Me—Jeannette Clift George, who told the Lord she would give him her life but would not give her public testimony or get involved in Bible classes or relate in any way in what was then called "religious drama." I now travel full-time and share my testimony, teach four Bible classes a week, and am the full-time director of a Christian theater company. I often wonder if it is wise to mention to the Lord, as well as other employers, what you will not do. However, I have found limitless joy in doing what I do and praise the Lord for his redirection.

Friends—An army of love recruited from Bible classes, theater, schools, church, neighborhood, and family.

One of my favorite Bible stories is the feeding of the five thousand. I see the disciples thinking Jesus must have lost his holy senses, telling them to feed the multitude when they didn't have so much as a gift coupon from McDonald's between them. And he kept saying it! How Peter must have worried, how Andrew must have puzzled, and how Thomas must have doubted. And then, in the midst of the quandary, this kid brings his leftover lunch! What possible good is that? It's leftovers from one lunch packed in the early morning and eaten during the day! Jesus took it and thanked God the Father for it because whatever God gives is always enough! So they fed the multitude and went on to the next day's miracle without thinking that what Jesus had done with the leftover lunch was enough reason for courage when they were lost in a storm at sea.

I identify with the kid who brought his leftover lunch. That's all I've got—the leftovers from the lunch of my life. I write from that. Hoping that from it, he may again feed the multitude.

CHAPTER 1

Connecting the Disconnected

Christmas and Easter tend to bookend the Christian faith, as well they should. The fact that the Word became flesh and that Word-indwelt flesh rose from the tomb marks the believer's life with sovereign assurance. However, the manger and the tomb have something in common. They are both empty. Christ arose most assuredly from that tomb and grew up and out of that manger. A baby, humanly helpless, and an entombed king would be easily manageable authorities. The vacant manger and tomb mean that the Lord who occupied them is not only alive and well but also in full and current authority. That is not always comfortable to us power-hungry human beings who expected the Lord we confessed, to stay politely ready for our haloed manipulations. And we also expected him to be quick in his answering of our often lengthy questions. The divine lull in his answers perplexes us. We give to God the tattered dressings of our humanity and assume his silence is similar to the glazed inattention we sometimes give others when we don't really care about the personalized story we're hearing in the grocery aisle. Sometimes, during awfully depressing times, we read his silence as more a criticism than inattention and a sign of broken fellowship or that there has never really been any fellowship at all.

The devil, with all of his wearying wiles and wickedness, delights in using any opportunity to get the believer to doubt his believership. The devil cannot separate us from the power of God, but he can make us doubt its contact. That doubt is a dangerous weed that can spoil the garden of the God we know. When the believer doubts his fellowship with God, the devil is satisfied! The evil one no longer has to tempt us with the delicacies of disobedience, for doubting the security of fellowship, we are in the devil's camp and available to his slightest command.

The question is, what do we do in the silences of God? What do we do when everyone else is getting daily telegrams, faxes, and DVDs directly from God, and our prayers bounce back from the ceiling of meditation without so much as a recorded message of closed office hours? How do we go on with the abundant life when there is an abundance of silence from the Resource Center from which we got life in the first place?

Well, my friend, I've been there. I've been there ringing the bell, pressing the golden buzzer, dialing the phone, crying through the window, and pressing my hands against my ears to drown out the thundering silence from God. I've outgrown the easy answers to questions I answered quickly for others and doubted the new answers will work in my difficult situation. I have tried to protect Almighty God from the facts of my hurt and keep smiling in his presence because nobody loves you if you're unhappy, certainly not God who asked us to enter his presence with thanksgiving. In the trenches of such reality, I have learned a working victory.

In the first place, God is sovereign! The God of the Genesis creation is sovereign, and by his sovereign choice he became a man. That's Christmas! Note the journey of the wise men following a star. Chart their long, long travel. Don't be fooled by Hallmark 5:3; it was no overnight trip and most probably not on camels but in a caravan of the finest horses. They came thundering through the streets of Jerusalem and demanded entrance unto Herod. They were driven by one surging need: they had lost sight of the star! All that long trip they had followed its gleaming, and now, nothing in the heavens, no signature of a signaling God, no pathway clearly marked.

Just like us, they went to the most likely human being, who in this case was the last person in the whole world to whom they should have told their story. Nevertheless, they had a meeting with Herod who had his own purposes in sending them on their way. Leaving Herod, looking up into the heavens, they saw it again—the star. The Bible says they rejoiced greatly! If you, like the wise men of old, are between stars, hold to your stance of faith. God will not leave you! His star for you is in the heavens! Wait for it. God's direction will surely come! But the wait may be a long, dry time between drinking fountains. Its silence may shake the assurance of faith and leave us with songs in the night that have no tune, no words, and no accompaniment.

I believe in the person of Jesus who is the Christ. I have believed in him for many years, but I can tell you honestly, I am not held to him by the strength of my unfaltering faith. I am held to him by the strength of his unfaltering grip on me! I sing the hymn with tears of joy, "Oh love that will not let me go! I rest my weary soul in Thee." It is his sovereign grip that holds me between the stars of his known guidance. And in his sovereign silence I have learned some principles.

In his silence:

> He is speaking volumes!
> He has the right to his mysteries.
> He will remind you of what he was saying when
>   he was talking.
> He invites you to state your requests specifically.
> He gives you valid ministry in the silence!
> He is sovereign.
> He is faithful.
> He loves you.

It happened in the Phoenix, Arizona, airport. I was changing planes while traveling on one airline which does not automatically transfer passenger luggage to another airline, and so I gathered my checked suitcase to carry it from one terminal to another. I asked a nearby attendant how to get to the second terminal, and when told the time of my flight, he answered with one word: Run! So I ran, lugging twice as much luggage as I needed for the trip, plus an overpacked purse over my arm and a small sack carrying the crossword puzzle magazine—which I had been unable to work on the first plane—and a hairbrush that I remembered at the last minute after I had locked my suitcase. I was not a pretty sight, but it got worse.

As I ran through terminal one, I realized my stride was slightly limited; and glancing down, I found my petticoat around my ankles! I knew I couldn't stop for proper repairs, so through the fabric of my skirt, with my elbow I gripped the petticoat's wavering elastic, scooted it up under my skirt, and still running, held it to the general area of my hip bone! This gave me a posture not before witnessed in the Phoenix airport, and passersby wanted to help, but they didn't know where to touch! It was hot, and perspiration joined my tears. I still had on all the makeup I had applied, but it was not where I had put it.

I made it to the shuttle transfer, through the checkpoint of the second plane, checked my luggage, and boarded the plane looking like a patient released in error from a hospital. I sat in the first available seat, overflowing the small space with carry-on clutter and critical concern. Hoping to find some semblance of ease, I opened the in-flight magazine so kindly pocketed in front of me. There was a picture of a traveler—tall, thin, wondrously attractive, and composed. One skimpy little purse hung from her well-postured shoulder. She had one small carry-on, carried with style in one small traveling carriage. She was stylish, neat, and young. (I may have been young when I started, but I couldn't remember.)

That picture of a traveler bore no resemblance whatsoever to the way I looked, and that picture was wrong! That's not the way travelers really look. I have looked carefully, and only a few short-distance travelers ever look neat. Travelers look hurried and harried and hindered by carry-ons, raincoats, babies and their standard equipment, handheld tickets, identification, and magazines. In fact, they look like I looked. So the picture was attractive but wrong! And if as a traveler I feel graded by that picture, I will never fully celebrate the trip!

Sometimes the Christian is so overloaded with pictures of Christian perfection that he doubts his belief, and Satan has a field day! Satan would rather have you and me doubting our relationship with God through Christ than actively involved in the most lurid sins. The action of sin is secondary to the absence of relationship, and without that relationship sin has no other course but its exercise. Desolate in the comparison of who we really are with who we think we ought to be, even the productive believer considers throwing in the towel, applying for immediate transfer or out-and-out resignation.

That false picture is never more disturbing than in the hours and circumstances when God seems to be silent. In that awesome quiet we trouble deaf heaven and shroud our soul in shame. The truth is that God is seldom, if ever, silent. He is the divine talker although he does find delight in dramatic pauses. In the apparent silences of God, know he is speaking volumes.

For the past few years I have done a daily radio show. It is a brief sharing of thoughts, but it takes preparation and a time set apart for the taping. For that period of taping, my office is turned into a studio. The telephone is unplugged, signs on the doors call for no interruption, messages posted in the hallway ask for silence, and we have brief prayer requesting a minimum of thunder or heavy trucks rolling by. The taping may take as much as an hour, and then the world outside my office returns to normal. Sometime during that normalcy I pick up my telephone to make a call. Almost without exception I let out a yelp of despair: my telephone doesn't work; the works have gone silent! My able and unperturbed assistant comes hurriedly into my office and reminds me that we disconnected my telephone. In order for it to work properly, we need to reconnect it.

In the silence of God, check your connection.

Certain matters may need your critical attention because they have blocked your contact with God and must be addressed before the one-to-one relationship can be restored—matters like bitterness, resentment, the various contrivances of self-centeredness, the deafness of concealed anger. The listing is limitless, but the general title is one simple word—sin!

Yes, sin. That same disconnection that Adam suffered in that first perfect garden now sends us hiding in the bushes like Adam did. I often find it disappointing to know there is no modern novelty in the matter of sin. It is the same break in communication, the same interruption of sweet fellowship, the same awkward separation that caused Adam and Eve, in hastily designed fig leaves, to hide shamefully amid the azaleas when great God Almighty went looking for them. The cowering couple make a sad picture, and so do we.

If it weren't for God, in the determination of grace, brushing aside branches and bushes and blushing blossoms to find Adam, there would be no hope for them or for us. God seeks the sinner. He offers fellowship through the finished work of Jesus. The gospel of Christ searches for fallen man as God did so long ago. All the calls of modern evangelism are nothing more or less than the seekings of God—seeking the one who has never accepted Christ to confess his sin, claim forgiveness, and grab his name tag for dining at the table of the King. And for the runaway Christian there is hope. I have been served it. I know its taste and offer that hope to any who assume God is silent when the silence is a matter of broken connection.

In the silence of God, first check the connection. Face God with confession! He yearns for fellowship even more than you do, and he has already paid the price for it. Not all the silences of God are the result of sin, but it is dangerous to overlook its possibility. If you are uncertain as to any disobedience in your life and yet there is the awesomeness of spaces in holy communication, ask God for clarification. In doing this, I advise you to sit down, for the answer may possibly be lengthy, as it has been with me. I also advise patience, not because God is hesitant in speaking but because listening is a fine art that needs time for realization.

What may be the sins that interfere with our communication with God? The Bible lists several and underlines ten of them. I mention a few that I have stumbled over: hidden anger, concealed envy, masked bitterness, a stubborn and unforgiving spirit so well packed in my daily carry-on that I can scarcely identify its specifics. Confession is simply agreeing with God, admitting right in the face of God that sin is sin and asking his forgiveness.

The matter of forgiving others is getting rid of the sticker burrs that haunt the tender undersoles of the runaway. Strangely enough, I have found it true that the one I refuse to forgive has a haunting authority over me and encourages the rapid growth of weeds in the garden of my daily life. We are to forgive others not because they deserve it but because it just happens to be in the top listing of God's commands. I have a choice to be in fellowship with bitterness or fellowship with God. Like any of the sins, it needs to be recognized, reckoned with, and relinquished.

I will never forget the moment in time when a truth-determined preacher spoke the words of 1 John 1:9. It was the evening service at a church in which I was a visitor. I heard the words and spoke a loud, "Oh." I was so occupied by the truth that I was not even embarrassed by my interruption of the service. That verse was the key unlocking a prison I thought was past invasion. I offer it with joy to any for whom that key might be the resolution for a godly silence.

Confess your sin. Believe that God has done what he said he would do when you did what he said for you to do! And get on with life! Don't make camp in the prison from which you have been released. You may, like our patriarch Jacob, still have a touch of arthritis in your right ankle, but it won't keep you from dancing to the music of the heavenlies.

One more thing before we go on to the other reasons for a silent God. I have found that the person most difficult to forgive is me. Myself. If God has forgiven you and you have not forgiven you, you are out of fellowship with God, and no hearing aid can overcome his silence. If you are still fighting off the mosquitoes of already-confessed sin, have a little talk with yourself. Is God's Word true? (It is.) Does he forgive as he said he would? (He does.) Would it not be better for you to agree with him? (It most certainly would!) Was he right to forgive you? (Probably not in your sight, but God is much more merciful than you and I are.) Does he deserve obedience? (You can

9

bet your life on it!) So forgive you, just because he did! Now celebrate!

There is a back door out of sin. The latchkey is a cross. It has never failed.

And now we can look at other principles that give hope to the wayfarer who troubles deaf heaven with his bootless cries and wonders if God is still speaking at all. (Indeed, he is.)

Dear God,

Thank you for speaking to me again. My ears are so used to silence I may miss a few words right at first, but now I'm happy to know you wanted to talk to me even more than I wanted to hear you. And thank you for paying the cost of having the connection restored; I could never have afforded it.

And Lord, while I am standing here in the grocery store aisle, please help this lady who is pouring out her life story to me. I don't know what I can do to help her with her complicated problem, but I know you already know the details she is breathlessly describing to me. Help me listen ahead of the pace of her words, and I would appreciate it if you would prompt my faltering memory as to how I know her and what I have done to receive this personal telling of her life's sad details. I think the problem is her brother's wife's cousin's son's boss. Please bless the people all along the line of the connection, and if you could take the time to keep frozen the frozen dinner in my shopping cart, I would greatly appreciate it.
Amen.

CHAPTER 2

Exits and Entrances

In the carefully detailed timing of God, I was in New York City when Dr. Billy Graham was holding an evangelistic crusade. It was in Madison Square Garden, and in that vast arena there were special sections designated for attendees who were working in or aspiring to be working in theater. I was part of that group who came from performance or rehearsal or classes or whatever we did to support our intention of classes, rehearsals, or performances. It was Dr. Graham's ardent belief that these showbiz types also deserved an opportunity to hear the gospel proclaimed. He encouraged the organizing of Christians in theater.

One aspect of that encouragement was a gathering held in a hotel room in which, after refreshments, the guests shared their testimonies. Most of the testimonies came from those whose decision for Christ had been made at those meetings in the Garden, and the details of lives lived without fellowship with Christ were, to say the least, colorful. I was hearing people telling of the giving up of things I didn't know anyone ever picked up. I had not been allowed to read magazines with such lurid details and was really enjoying learning about scandalous behavior while I was in a reverent atmosphere.

I praise the Lord for my testimony of relationship with him, but my testimony paled in comparison with the ones I was hearing. In fact, my personal testimony has only one dramatic highlight and is actually dull. As the group shared their experiences, I became increasingly uncomfortable. I, too, was an entertainer, but my personal script did not qualify as a shocking crowd pleaser. As the circle of confessors got nearer to me, I reminded the Lord that my testimony lacked histrionics. Could I tell someone else's when my turn came? God did not take kindly to that idea, and I wondered if when they called my name I could feign a faint and let them wonder what mine would have been. That was not acceptable either. I turned to a young man sitting beside me with his head in his hands. The young man was a musician of great promise, but at the moment he looked as unpromising as I did. I whispered to him, "Soon it will be my turn, and my testimony is not dramatic. In fact, I grew up in a Christian home. My father is a Baptist deacon!" The young man beside me said, "How do you think I feel? My father is a Methodist preacher!"

I shared my testimony, and the young man beside me shared his. Nobody cried, nobody applauded, nobody's life was changed—except mine and maybe my new friend's. I learned the highest drama of a testimony happened on a cross, and any claiming of that has its own unique story.

Several years ago my husband and I were on the island of Granada. I was part of a group of Christian artists brought to perform for the citizenry of that exquisite island. We were painters, pianists, singers, and performers who had been called to join the missionaries because someone in high and artistic places had reckoned with the power of the believer artist's voice.

It was an enormous and fulfilling honor. The natives of that Caribbean oasis of beauty attended in full-throated delight. Many of them walked miles barefoot to enjoy our programming. I was also to speak at a local church and give my testimony. My husband and I enjoyed worshipping with the small congregation before I was introduced, and then suddenly my enjoyment was interrupted by the fact that my testimony springs from the dilemma of depression and anxiety, and there upon those peaceful and calm faces, I saw no tracings of such concerns. The people of Granada take time to live their lives in gentleness. What would they know of my experience?

I whispered to my husband, "My testimony won't mean anything to these people."

He put his arm around me and whispered, "But you will."

His comfort was appreciated but not helpful. I searched faces to find some sign of those silent sorrows I had known and found none. And then I was introduced! As I walked to the platform, I left my notes behind. I did not speak of my agonizing pilgrimage. I spoke only of Christ—of his love, of his cross, and of his lordship. The people responded. Decisions were even made. The Christian experience depends upon him who is truth. The experience may have numberless variations. His truth is one as he is. I have been privileged to speak in many areas of this country and in several international programs, but I have never seen this request to vary. The people say, "Sirs (or, Madam, as the case may be), we would see Jesus."

I grew up in a Christian home, for which I will be eternally grateful. The practices of the church were routine to me, and when I was twelve years old, I walked down the aisle to profess my faith in Jesus. My mother was transferring her letter to that church membership, and I followed her with my own stammering statement of belief. My father came behind me, and he and I were baptized together. A momentous beginning.

So long as I stayed in the church, I never questioned its routine and respected the wisdom and calling of the pastors in our pulpits. I stayed comfortably with a chapel program in the first two years of college; and then, majoring in theater, I was no longer active in church participation. By the time I got to New York to become a professional actress, I viewed God from a distance.

From a distance I had many questions that my own memory of church teaching did not answer. I was drawn to the periphery of cults, often enthusiastically involved in philosophical discussions of some higher being's unattainable positioning, and claimed an enlightenment that simplified the faith of my family to an insignificant status. I believed God had something to do with creation but was currently uninvolved with his creation and, most especially, me. If I called myself a Christian, it was without the capital letter; but the ritual of my childhood held, and I attended some church service weakly and weekly, choosing carefully that which was distant from my childhood practice.

My theater activity increased, which should have made me happy, satisfied, and at ease with the world and its dispositions. It did not. I became depressed, deeply depressed. No one knew it. I was a clever actress and covered my despair well. Then a friend gave me a stack of books to read, and one was Phillips's translation of the Epistles, with which I was unfamiliar. Since the book did not say "Bible" on its cover, I did not recognize the source of wisdom from which I was reading. However, God's Holy Word does not require recognition in order to be relevant.

Literally from the Word of God, I reckoned with the Lord absent in my life but fully sovereign in his. And all alone in my apartment, I relinquished the leadership of my life to the lordship of Jesus. It was a major change. This was before the Billy Graham Crusade, and I had no Christian fellowship conducting my adjustment to this change in my life. And I whimpered in the newness of prayer that I, an adult, was spiritually bankrupt. I had no investment upon which to build. I had no faith to enjoy maturity. I had nothing accredited to my account. And God said, "Oh yes, you do." "He is able to guard what has been entrusted to me" (2 Tim. 1:12). And there on my account statement registered by my most holy God was my little twelve-year-old confession of faith. Kept by God against that day.

Suffering in God's silence is often a shortsighted dilemma. We see only in the small circles of hopeless reasoning. We hear only what has been preset by our conviction of defeat. It takes a deliberate choice to free our awareness from its stupor of despondency.

> Open my eyes that I may see
> Glimpses of truth Thou hast for me;
> Place in my hands the wonderful key
> That shall unclasp and set me free:
> Open my ears that I may hear
> Voices of truth Thou sendest clear;
> And while the wave-notes fall on my ear,
> Everything false will disappear.
>   —CLARA H. SCOTT

As I hum that dear old hymn, "Open My Eyes, That I May See," I sense again how deeply we need the old hymns with the ever-fresh words of wisdom. I don't remember being smart enough to sing those words years ago, locked in the fallacy of my nothingness, but I encourage the consideration of that statement of seeking.

The Scripture tells us of Lazarus, freed from the grave, still wrapped in the entrapment of grave clothes. Jesus, whose voice had called Lazarus from the tomb, now gave direction to those standing thunderstruck at Lazarus' reentry into life. That direction from the Christ may be unto the work of the community of faith today. Encourage the one recovered to activate his senses unto the processing of life! That is the goal of my own testimony. Broadcasting the return of the prodigal that we may not only leave the pigpens to the pigs but also celebrate the investment of the Father who never closed the account!

Someone got me into the Word of God, and there was my release from spiritual bankruptcy!

> In the silence of God, risk a wider view.
> See what your God has kept for you.

In the silence of God, look back to what he once said.

If you wandered out of the circuit of his will, you may have to go back to the place where you got out to get back into the place you should be. To affirm that action, go back to the place you first got in. The Word of God still holds. His promise has not changed. That's why I sing "O Love That Wilt Not Let Me Go!" That is why, even in the silence of God, I know God's grip on me will not slacken its hold. I am not held by my faith in him; I am held by his grip on me. My faith, in its exercise, reveals that grip and assures me of its security. In the silence of God, look back to the place where you got in: its predicate is still true.

I was being driven to Seattle from the airport. In front of us was a large motorbike with a man hunkered down, driving against the wind. Behind him was a small child whom I assumed to be his son and a car behind them that had, what seemed to be, a watching mother at the wheel.

We passed the motorbike, and to my astonishment I noted that there were no safety belts holding the child to the driver, no guard seat behind his small back. The only thing holding the child was his childish grip on the driver's leather jacket! Although they traveled safely and turned off to a roadside park after we passed them, I said aloud to my friend, "What a frightening thing. That child's security depended on his little fingers gripping his daddy's leather jacket. Little fingers in the cold lose their clutch, and leather gets slippery in the wind. What kind of father would entrust his child to so weak a grasp?" And there beside my friend I gasped, and tears came unexpectedly. That was what I had thought was my safety in God—dependent on my grip on him! No wonder I was frightened by the trip, uneasy in my travel, and sickened by God's silence. For if it's up to me, safe I will never be! It is not my grip on him; it is his grip on me.

In the silence of God, look back to where you got in! His promise holds! Dip into Hebrews 13:5; God is speaking volumes: "I will never leave you or forsake you."

And then perhaps another focus is in order. In the silence look back and then look ahead! My husband and I attended a church service when we were first casually dating. He followed me into the church, and I slipped into a backseat row where I saw two seats available. I am a back-row person and was pleased to find those seats. I mumbled excuses toward the people whose knees I endangered, and comfortably seated, I looked to see my escort settle into the seat beside me. He was not there. He was not beside me. He was not behind me waiting in the aisle. I was confused. He was not where he was supposed to be, and then, looking ahead, I saw him standing, smiling down in front—from a front row—and pointing to two available seats. I had a significant choice that caused me some embarrassment as I moved from the back row, but in that moment I learned three things:

1. This kind, patient, and tenderhearted gentleman whom I would in time happily marry would not always follow my directions.

18

2. Front-row seats are really excellent seats.
3. Sometimes the leader is neither beside nor behind you but ahead of you—waiting.

In the silence of God, look ahead.

He may have preceded you in the action of his sovereign guidance and found not only better placement but an easy way to teach you to keep focused on him, even in his silences.

Working in Washington, D.C.'s Arena Theater, I was playing the role of Major Barbara in George Bernard Shaw's noble play *Major Barbara*. I relished the opportunity, loved the play, and was delighted to be working with enormously gifted people, most of whom went on to established and highly successful careers. Two lines within that play held rich meaning for me at the time it was played but have increased in value as lifetime experience has underlined their meaning. I did not say the lines. They were said to me—by Phil Bosco, one of the great actors of our day. Phil, in his character, looked at me, as his dispirited daughter Barbara, and said, "You have learnt something. That always feels at first as if you had lost something." It is true. New learning feels at first as though something has been lost. And it has. To learn and claim some new thing, we generally have to give up that which the new has corrected or at least change its priority.

Recently I went to a podiatrist. I thought I had sprained my foot. I learned that I was wearing shoes a size smaller than my foot was measuring. I didn't know feet continue to grow after the rest of us is grown up! I fancy myself that weight has nothing to do with it! The new thing I had learned would have serious effect on the shoes I was wearing! It worked! I gained freedom from a limp and a sore back. But I also lost something; my old shoes had to be replaced with the new.

Learning the sovereignty of God introduces a deep readjustment of all that has been sovereign. We have to give up that which the new has corrected or at least demote its positioning. Error can be comforting. It is false comfort and difficult to get rid of! So long as those old shoes stay in the far corner of my closet, they will occasionally call to me to try them one more time.

Memo

One thing I don't need any more of is wire coat hangers. They invade my house like mosquitoes after a summer rain. They come in camouflaged by jackets and dresses from the cleaners. They slip out of shirts and blouses and hide in the corners of my closet. They multiply by some weird habits of breeding in my winter storage and parade their newborn young each spring and summer. A creative friend of mine covered them with banded fabric and gave them as Christmas presents, but I knew them for what they were and never used them! You can hang things from them, bend them into shapes, and open the locked windows of your car, but except for such unreliable emergencies, they don't do any good thing after you have piled every garment you have in the house over them and still have half a closet full of them left over! The cleaners don't want them back, Goodwill won't accept boxes of them, and if you try giving a friend a sweater with two wire hangers in it, the friend slips them out from the sweater and returns them to you.

The fact is that life has a lot of things in it that you don't want any more of and have too much of right now. Sorry, that's life. Give the quality of the good authority over the quantity of the bad, and fret not over the wire hangers.

Oh, God, let the wire hangers remind me of the good things on which I can hang each morning—the out-of-style black suit that fashion has just welcomed again, the shoes I bought on sale that fit really well, the white slacks I mistakenly washed with the blue shirt and now make, with the blue shirt, a matching ensemble. There is more good than bad in my closet, so I mustn't get hung up on the hang-ups. There is more to life than wire hangers.

The silence of God may need to be addressed by his holy positioning and sometimes the discovery that we have altered his definition to suit our own design. God is not God because he is good; God is God because he is God. He defines his goodness by himself, not himself defined by our definition of good. God is good. The gentleness of God, which is true; the kindness of God, which is true; the unfaltering love of God, which is true; in no way alter the authority of his leadership. He leads. We follow. Racing ahead of God is disastrous! Running too far behind him is debilitating. Running with him is energizing. He leads. We follow.

God is God, and I am not!

Even in the abundance of God so loving the world, even in the limitless bounty of his grace, only once and once only do God and man change places. God who became man to save us, became as man to redeem us, to pay the price for our redemption! But only once.

Other than that awesome juxtaposition, God is always God, the authoritative sovereign leader; and we, with all the loving care of God, are never more than man, God's choicest creation. Recognizing that divine authority means we give up something of our own, the dictum of our own will, the claiming of our own way, and the relinquishing of our own wisdom.

I do not equate my husband with God, but the example of the change in seating at that church brings up a light-hearted illustration of a godly principle. One of God's choicest blessings to me has been a happy marriage, a romantic marriage, a productive marriage, and a marriage filled with all things good. I had quite a collection of single years before I married, and the changes in the processing of blissful and mutual leadership were not always easy.

My husband and I visited New York City shortly after we were married. I had lived in that wondrous town for many years. Our first evening there we left for the theater, and each of us hailed a cab! And both of them came! It was not a major problem, but one couple with two hailed cabs requires a decision resulting in one lesson for one independent wife and one angry cab driver.

It is my choice to detour the sensitive matter of submission, however I need to explain one aspect of it. I did not give my husband authority; his authority came with the packaging of him. No two marriages are alike, and not all husbands have natural authority. Mine did. My husband also loved me with more tenderness than that sung in the sweetest of ballads, and I knew it. In the middle of a New York

City street, I made a leadership adjustment and tried not to gloat when my husband did not know how to tip a New York cabbie, and I counted out the money for him to select the proper amount.

Now the principle of God's sovereign authority is never dimmed, denied, or distracted by his encompassing love. The contemporary grace-flourishing Christian needs to be reminded of that. The ways of the Lord are right. God is good! He is not trying to attain goodness by pleasing us. He is good! He is not good because he does what we consider good. What he does is good because he is God, and God is good. When we tally up God's daily actions to prove whether he is good, we may often find ourselves awash in his silence. God does not bargain, he does not negotiate, and he does not take orders very well. When he says, "Come, let us reason together," he doesn't always mean what I mean by "reasoning."

As artistic director of a Christian theater company, I meet many crises. One of those crises directed me to call a sudden prayer meeting in our chapel. The leaders of the various groups joined me as we crowded solemnly into the little room that shares library, study, and quick nap times with its praying prerogatives. I briefly outlined the strategy of our prayers and, with bowed head and wavering voice, prayed in this manner, "Dear Lord, This need is so great, this problem is so immediate, this crisis is so mysterious, I don't know what to tell you to do about it!"

Praying eyes opened suddenly, gazing at me, and I heard what I had prayed! Once again God tapped me on the shoulder and said, "Let us review the casting: me, God; you, Jeannette." I can't do God's work, and he knows it. When I forget it, he reminds me.

There are times in the silence of God when I do not hear him speak because I have tried to place him in a position he does not occupy—a position under my authority, waiting to do my will. I am learning that, although he will not let me go because he promised and his eye is still on me because he promised—to me as well as to the wavering sparrow—his voice is heard from his sovereign positioning. I must look back to the place where he was sovereign and still is, and look forward to the place where he will still be sovereign.

God is good! His way is right! And maybe, just maybe, he seems to be silent because our ears are not yet tuned to the voice of his authoritative leadership.

In the silence his guidance can be seen as the view from your rear window, and you can trust him on that premise! His guidance also may be seen from his positioning ahead of you, and you can trust him on that promise. But premise or promise, his is the voice of lordship.

Memo

Sometimes I feel like a cloison. In the first place, a lot of people don't even know what I am. A cloison is a metal enclosure with enamel painted on it, which doesn't have much value. The fact that it is an early art form with a wonderful heritage doesn't mean much to one isolated partition of wire and fading color. However, when that cloison connects to other cloisons, it becomes part of an artistic statement that brings joy and décor to people's lives, gets honored in museums, holds flowers or cherished treasures, serves fruit attractively placed, or fills a corner of the room gathering dust and compliments.

The cloison-to-cloison connection is the result of a master designer who secures the little cloisons into a basic metal object unto a pattern satisfying to the creator who saw in each little cloison significant potential. A cloison cannot connect itself, design itself, or move unaided into placement within the wire strips of various stations.

However, a cloison can accept the coloring of enamel, fit cozily into the designer's placement, shine in its place, and even wait wherever it's placed, knowing the master designer never overlooks one cloison and always has a pattern for it to complete.

Sometimes I feel like a cloison, and that's not really a bad thing at all when you consider who the Master Designer is.

CHAPTER 3

The Flight of the Butterfly

*M*ost of my adult life has been spent in theater. In fact, it started when I was eight years old and my mother took me to see a touring production of the opera *Madame Butterfly*. From the moment the curtains opened, I wanted to be part of the world behind the footlights. More than anything else in my world, I wanted to be a beautiful Japanese lady who sang a lot. I never made all that, but I did become an actress. I enjoy theater and respect it.

It has been my privilege to play a variety of roles that include significant women who made enormous contributions to our culture, to our history, and to our communities. Among them were Julian of Norwich, Eleanor Roosevelt, Ruth Graham, the dowager empress of Russia, and of course

Corrie ten Boom. To play these women of great heroic character, I had to stretch to reach their nobility. My way into their
character was to find some menial attribute with which I could
identify and build from that unto their greatness. For Ruth
Graham, I chose her sense of humor; for the dowager empress,
her sense of history; and for Corrie, her love of family.

The heroes of Scripture afford me the same entry points,
a low point for entry that I might gain application from the
high points of their produce. For instance, the great and grand
prophet Elijah. He took on the prophets of Baal and won the
contest on Mt. Carmel. He, in the name of sovereign God, hum-
bled the posture of a nation's idol worship, brought fire from
sodden wood, rain from dry-eyed heaven, and recognition of
Jehovah from pagan lips. The least he expected in return was a
complimentary breakfast, but instead his life was threatened by
the queen, a lady of dubious distinction who won King Ahab's
hand and, with it, led the heart of Israel away from Jehovah and
into destruction.

I do not have Elijah's courage. I have not stood on a
mountaintop deriding a huge crowd of pagan priests and seen
God weave water and fire together for a major miracle. I cannot make easy contact with Elijah's highest moments, but I can
touch the tattered hem of his prophet's robe when he crouched
beneath a juniper tree and cried out to God in the depths of
despair. I know what it's like to be wearied into quitting. I know
what it's like to have my best efforts disregarded by the very
people for whom I did what I thought was best. I know what
it's like to render unto God my letter of resignation and have
him circle the misspelled words and send it back to me. There

was Elijah, heartbroken, seeking solace from God and hearing nothing. The silence of God.

I know what the silence of God sounds like to ears numbed by despair. And I know the speaking of God beyond the sounds and beyond the silence. God was speaking volumes to Elijah, but depression had paralyzed the prophet's eardrums, and he almost didn't hear God at all. But God kept speaking!

If we are not attentive, we, too, will let God's *no* drown out God's *yes*. God's *no* always, always opens a path for his *yes*. Always! Always! As I write these words, I initial them with my own Elijah tears! It was not Elijah's quitting that was the wrong thing to do. Sometimes quitting under grace is the best of choices. But Elijah's reason for quitting was his error. Elijah gave God four reasons for resigning, and they were all wrong:

1. Elijah did his best, and it was not recognized.
2. Elijah thought God's assignment could not be done!
3. Elijah thought the whole plan of God depended on Elijah!
4. Elijah thought he would do better than those who preceded him. He thought he, Elijah, could correct all the errors of his history. (I find this one particularly embarrassing.)

Well, the truth of the matter is that items 4, 3, 2, and 1 were never in the God-given listing of Elijah's assignments. However, they are all common to most of us human-being types fretting over the silence of God who did not consider the top four of our problems any of our business!

Number 4—Elijah thought he would do better than those who preceded him. We may be called to protect our history, but

I am unaware of a call to correct our history. With the premium blessing of learning from our predecessors, we occasionally congratulate ourselves when we make better choices than they, but more often experience humbles us and makes us less critical and more compassionate. Teenagers generally know exactly what their parents are doing wrong and frequently communicate this advanced knowledge. Those same teenagers grow up and become parents and find themselves not only understanding what their parents did but often repeating it.

I am now artistic director of a large and productive Christian theater company. I purposed to correct with deeper understanding the errors of some artistic directors under whom I have worked. But instead of correcting their errors, I now see the reasons for their choices, and my criticism of them has turned to compassion for them! I have picked up many a task thinking I could do better than what I saw previous taskmasters doing less than well. Time and again, I have learned that it was not the taskmaster that limited the assignment's effectiveness but the task itself.

Any leader is subject to criticism—helpful and loving or negative and mean. It comes from the territory of leadership. The distance between the leader and the follower is often more of experience than expertise, more of information than appointment, and strangely enough requires mutual respect to produce good results. When the follower becomes a leader, the previous leader's record is a bounty of helpfulness. But if the new leader believes his first assignment is to better the previous record, his only hope is a talent for shock resisting.

God's goal is unique to each follower. He tailors the assignment for the gifts he has given, and the new leader's first assignment is always unto personal obedience to the sovereign God. This sovereign God may change the task for the new leader, but this same sovereign God knows how different the same task looks when seen from inside the mantle of leadership.

My husband came into our marriage with an excellent driving record. He could park any sized car, drive steadily for hours, and his only recorded violation was for his failure to put sufficient money into the meter when we went to get our marriage license! However, soon after our wedding, it seemed necessary for me to assist his driving by a running commentary of advice. On our way to church, for instance, I pointed out to him the turns in the traffic, the driveways for which he needed to be alerted, the proper lane for turning onto the freeway (which, incidentally, he had built), and the speed of any approaching car. This guidance continued without much response on his part throughout our marriage. Then there came a time when he became ill, and it was necessary for me to drive. Now I was at the wheel on our way to church, and he, sitting beside me, resumed the same pattern of advice I had practiced—pointing out the turns in the traffic, the driveways, etc. You see, he who sitteth beside the wheel thinketh he hath more understanding than he who sitteth behind it.

Do you find God silent because you are stricken with the deafening remorse of not doing better than your mentors—or parents or teachers or directors or even prophets? It may be that the reason he says nothing about the assignment you failed is because he had nothing to say about the assignment you claimed. Perhaps he did not call you to set the old record straight but to make the new record totally his. Maybe your new position needs more compassion than comparison, and he has much to say about that.

Number 3—Elijah thought the whole plan of God depended on Elijah. When I married, I was not a young bride. My husband had enjoyed for many years a happy marriage with his first wife, who had died. He and I were arranging our wedding in the midst of two mature schedules, and he had cleared a break in his work while I found mine more resistant to interruption. My pastor, Dr. James Riley, met with us a few weeks before our wedding and asked of our plans for a wedding trip. My husband-to-be stammered a bit, and I explained that I was teaching three classes and maintaining speaking engagements while directing our theater company. Dr. Riley smiled at me and said, "Jeannette, if this marriage means to you what I think it does, you should clear a little more time for its celebration." And then, holding my hand across his desk, he said to me the startling words, "Jeannette, God has others!"

I was stunned. My husband-to-be was pleased. And we planned a lovely wedding trip.

Elijahs of the world, work with the focus of one upon whom God depends but know in your heart, God has others.

Aloneness is often a fact of reality and not to be dismissed by vagrant philosophy or the cheer of Hallmark cards. It is possible for the Christian life to be lived, and even abundantly, without ever knowing another believer! The life of the Christian rests on the person and finished work of the Christ, but oh my friends and fellows in the faith, our numbers are legion. Don't be fooled. There are more of us worshipping in churches than attending the Super Bowl! There are more of us on mission fields than on the unsettled thrones around the world! God has his kids everywhere.

Our theater company presented one of our shows in New York City, and it was for us a major program. We were advised to challenge Gotham with a play of more general market value than Christian statement. So we did a production of our play *John, His Story,* which is a clearly stated and staged retelling of the Gospel of John. We knew it would not hit a wave of popularity. I went to New York for the opening, and one night our promotional director assigned me to an interview on a popular all-night radio talk show. I asked if the show were secular and was told it most certainly was. I was told it would be of great marketing value, even though we would be broadcast between one and two a.m. I was reluctant to do the show knowing that secular talk-show hosts can be critical of Christian programmers, especially at 1:00 in the morning. It was decided that our show's director, Lee Walker, would be with me (the playwright and producer), and we were repeatedly reminded that this was a secular radio show.

Our business is theater. The fact that it is a Christian theater focuses its intention with a Christian signature, but theater is theater. What did we do to be accepted on a secular program? We practiced being relaxed, thinking slouching might look secular! We tried to think of secular phrases to incorporate in our conversation, but decided we didn't know what they meant and might not find them appropriate! I had quit smoking years ago but thought I could pick it up for the interview if I could overcome the fit of coughing with secular sophistication. Waiting outside the studio, we decided to give each other a certain look if one of us thought the other was not sufficiently secular for the program.

When we were ushered into the studio, Joey, the host, waved to us without interrupting his highly paced comments. There we sat for about thirty minutes. I decided this secular program had us there for a joke and would dismiss us without an interview. No, there was no dismissal. Instead, the host said, "We have with us tonight two who came all the way from Texas to bring their theater to us. I guess they thought we needed a little help from Texas here in the big city!" Lee and I shivered at the thought of what would next be said. "Well," Joey said, "I saw the show tonight." Lee and I glanced at each other, and I measured the paces to the nearest door. "Yes, I saw their little show tonight," Joey continued, "and as a born-again believer, I encourage you to see it. If you're a Christian, you will enjoy its truth; if you are not a Christian, come to see this fine show and find out what the Christian's joy is all about!" Born-again believer! Did Joey not know his show was secular?

Lee and I were as statues! Joey turned to me and said, "And you are the writer?" I answered with all the assurance of a five-year-old at his first trip to the ice cream parlor. "Yes, I am." Then Joey turned the mike to Lee and said, "And you are the director?" And Lee nodded. It was radio, and Lee nodded! "Born-again believer!" Yes, Joey knew his market, but he also knew his Master! God has his kids everywhere!

Hear that, Elijah! Hear that, Jeannette! Hear that, trembling, despairing believer lost in the silence of solitude. God has others!

Don't let the world fool you. We not only have witnesses positioned in the heavenlies but also placed everywhere. Joey serving his ministry behind a microphone. The check-out clerk at my grocery store. A parole officer, a noted scientific lecturer, weathermen, landscape designers, pilots, teachers, judges, lawyers, bank presidents, ministers of little churches in Uganda, philosophers, emergency room doctors, garbage collectors—all positions and all cultures, and yes, even actors and actresses and writers and editors.

God's got lots of choices, and here's the miracle: He chose you, Elijah, not because you were all he had but because you were the one he wanted. He chose me not because I was all he had but because I was the one he wanted. He chose you, beloved reader, not because you were all he had but because you were the one he wanted to do the job assigned.

And that should settle Elijah's reasons numbers 1 and 2, but it usually doesn't.

CHAPTER 4

*Help Wanted,
Applause Needed*

When God speaks through the silence, he often has a lot to say.

There was Elijah, whimpering under a juniper tree, explaining to God why quitting seemed an advantageous thing to do, and quitting for all the wrong reasons. Now I don't know that Elijah's reasons were wrong! This was a great man of God whose work has stood for generations. It was Elijah who joined Moses in accompanying Christ at his transfiguration. I don't know that Elijah whimpered or whined or wasted an opportunity, but I do know that when I read of his letdown from the upgrade of Mt. Carmel, I see my doubts illustrated. I see in his experience truths for my enlightenment. And I see in his reasons flaws that eat away the rationale of mine, like hungry moths feasting on my wool sweater, which I meant to put away with mothballs but thought I would get to it later.

Elijah's first two reasons for quitting were simple.

Number 2—Elijah wanted to quit simply because he thought the job could not be done. This may be a good reason for quitting except when you are under the assignment of God. If you are under the assignment of God, quitting because you think the job can't be done is the second worst reason you can offer.

I may have misread my assignment, I may have picked up somebody else's job by mistake, I may have rushed out into obedience before I heard the whole message, I may have overestimated my abilities, but if this whole thing is God's assignment, I can be sure it can be done! Because he will get it done! "He who started a good work in you will carry it on to completion" (Phil. 1:6).

The Bible tells us an interesting story about three men who didn't quit. Their reasons for staying at their post were better than Elijah's were for quitting. David the king was finishing the hard-fought terms of his reign. He took time to honor the mighty men who had loyally followed him. In that list are the names and heroic accounts of three men who served David with special fervor. I know nothing about who they were, but I am deeply impressed by what they did.

One man won! He won his battle! He was victor! Winners are to be honored. In fact, their honors shed a little light on the dim arenas of those who lose! In our compassion for the losers, don't forget to celebrate the winners. This man, of David's most honorable men, won! I haven't won often. I have a tendency to lose more than I win, but I most earnestly hope that I will never lose my enthusiasm for winning by sulking over losing. David's first most honorable man won!

I was nominated for a Golden Globe Award. I was so excited. My husband and I went to the big event in Hollywood. The place was packed. When the nominees were announced, huge flashing spotlights brushed the auditorium, and I stood up as an honored nominee. Of course, the nationwide broadcasting had a commercial break while I stood up, so no one at home saw me, but I stood there! I thought it was wonderful! It was for the film *The Hiding Place.* Its enormously gifted director, Jimmy Collier, and his wife, Emmy, were at our table. It was a wonderful event. I did not win; but I cheered the winner and thanked God for being in the circle of chosen ones from whom the winner was selected.

After the event, all of the nonwinning nominees were gathered together for a picture and for a meeting with Debbie Reynolds. I was having a wonderful time. I visited with some friends whom I had known while working in New York who had gone on to fame and stardom. Lots of faces of people whose names I did not remember came by to see me and congratulate me. Then Debbie Reynolds, who is a dear and gracious person, spoke to us. She encouraged us. She said she had never received a Golden Globe nomination and for us to be pleased with our honor. I was already pleased with my honor and thanked God for the little Styrofoam replica of the golden statue. I still keep that replica on my shelf. I was delighted, and then Debbie said that we, the losers, were all winners! And everyone applauded.

I am simplistic. We weren't all winners. The winners got little golden statues and were off in another room being interviewed by the press! Winners win, or there would be no honors in the contest! My little replica of the golden figurine is precious because of the golden figurine I didn't get. I was honored. I never felt left out. I felt counted in because I was part of the circle from which winners won!

Don't begrudge the winner! His honors shed light on all those who participate. One of David's most honored men was honored because he won! Whatever the price, whatever it took, he won. Hooray for the winners who honor the King. Winning to honor the King is a good reason to stay at your post.

Then one of David's most honored men stood his ground in the middle of a lentil field! He fought for David and took his stand. It wasn't at the head of a parade, it wasn't on the bandstand, it wasn't in the winner's circle; it was in the midst of a field of lentils. An ordinary bean field! And there he fought, and David knew it and honored him. Battles often are joined in unlikely places. War finds its own nests. Spiritual battles are often fought in ordinary fields, without flags and trumpets and marching bands. But this man fought where the battle found him. And there he took his stand for the king. God makes no mistakes in his placements. Where he put me is the place to take my stand, and where he put you is the place to take your stand!

The third of David's most honored mighty men really touches my heart. I thrill to the tune of the winner, and I wave my flag in honor of the one who took his stand, but this third man feeds my soul in a unique way. This man fought when he was so weary he could scarcely hold his sword, and he didn't quit. I repeat a truth I don't want to dismiss: often quitting is the best, the wisest, the most honorable thing to do. God has others to take our place, fill the gap, and keep the show on the road. We are not singularly essential to the plan of God, but we are accountable for commitment. Weariness is not always wisdom, but it is not always a good excuse for withdrawal. Don't linger too long in the battle, but don't quit too soon. Protect your options: you can quit tomorrow, but if you quit today, you lose your option for quitting tomorrow. I would say to that valiant man—weaving in his weary steps, sword held so loosely he can no longer grasp it properly, forcing his eyes to see through the cloudings of despair—"Hail to you, valiant warrior!" All the wiles of strategy were lost in weakness, all the tactics of battle training were melted in the sweat of muscles pushed past their limits, the schooling of discipline had been drained away; but he didn't quit. He still stood and fought in obedience to his king.

Elijah wanted to quit because he thought God's assignment couldn't be done. When I want to quit, that's why I want to quit. When I want to give up, that's why I want to give up. Who wants to die for a losing cause? If the job can't be done, I want out of it; but if it can be done, I want to be in it!

And now we have to face Elijah's first reason for quitting.

Number 1—Insufficient recognition when I'm doing the best I can! This is a problem for parents, teachers, leaders, etc. *You will not get all the recognition you deserve from children, students, followers.* Oh, you'll get some of it now, and a lot of it later; but as for now, you'll not get as much as you want and maybe not even as much as you need. If that's the only supply of resource to keep you going, you are in real trouble. It's not the recognition from your followers that you can depend on; it's the recognition from your leader. And when our Leader is silent, we start trying to make up the difference from lesser sources.

> notallbranchesgrowclosetothefruitbutallbranches-
>   growclosetothevine!
> Not all branches grow close to the fruit,
> but all branches grow close to the vine.

In the silence of God, when you are doing the best you can without the proper recognition from the ones you are serving, thank the Lord for his trust in you. He trusted you to serve without seeing the fruit. In fact, you may never see the fruit in this garden. But if you're growing close to the vine, you are bearing fruit, because of the fruit-growing power of the vine. When you and I live close to the vine, we may not catch a glimpse of the fruit, which is a little disappointing, but close to the vine all tears are turned into apple juice or peach nectar or maybe even a little grape wine, depending on our denomination of choice.

You can call a meeting of those insensitive ones whom you serve and address them as follows: "Dear Children (or students or followers), I am doing the best I can, and I am deeply saddened by the lack of recognition I get from you. I have prepared your meals (offered extra hours in study hall, shown you a better way), and my cup now runneth over with need. I need to know that you care (that you are learning, that you are progressing) and would deeply appreciate some indication from you that will encourage me."

In closing you might lead them in prayer, or erase the black-board, or take a coffee break. As you leave the room, you will glance back at the most bewildered group of people the world has ever known. They had no idea of your needs and will not understand them until they are parents (teachers, or leaders), at which time you may get a greeting card, an apple, or a watch.

This page can be photocopied and posted or given appropriately as the reader decides:

Informational Bulletin

Parents, Teachers, Leaders (add your category if not properly listed) occasionally need tender loving care. Statistically speaking, they are doing the best they can. One word of thanks from you, one note of compliment, one gesture of encouragement, could make all the difference in the world.

Thank you.

Memo

The white-cheeked, small-billed chickadee, weighing a third of an ounce, is an astonishing creature. In the midst of the snow and ice and blustering winds of winters in Maine, this little creature sings merrily a song of survival amid the harshest of conditions.

Survival is something well worth singing about. There is something deeply wonderful about being still there when circumstances seem to move like a well-aimed arrow with you as the target. God's gifts and provisions are generally in abundance, but there are times when the finishing line of one particular race is met with scarcely enough breath remaining to announce a victory. But the victory is no less meaningful because of the scarcity of its margin.

Sometimes we need to be prompted by the small-billed chickadee. He made it through the temperatures that defied his existence. I have never heard that little creature's song in the tempest of Maine's blow-hard weather, but I have sensed his triumph in small winnings in the empowering of God. Lavish victory is a lavish blessing, but so is victory in the merest second of its resolution. Survival is the ultimate challenge. There are moments when that in itself is grace and needs to have its song sung above the chatter of defeated circumstances.

So perhaps you did not win the gaudiest trophy, and perhaps you did not sail easily into the winners' circle, and perhaps you did not have the extra energy to dance once around the track; but by the grace of the living God, you survived, and today is a splendid day for a song. The little chickadee knows what he is singing about, and so do you and I.

CHAPTER 5

A Well-Weathered Bookmark

Meanwhile, back at the juniper tree. We find Elijah, down-hearted, weary, committed to quitting, but tenderly loved by God. God loved him. No one understands rejection better than God, and he had great compassion for his prophet. God sent an angel to his troubled prophet. The angel was specific; God's messengers often are. On his way to the juniper tree, the angel stopped by the corner grocery and bought a little cake and bottled water and told Elijah to eat and drink. Now there is the detailed and delicate attention of God. Sometimes our greatest need is simply met.

God is like my neighbor across the street. She has crossed the distance of our little street and brought cookies and cakes to my house just when I most deeply needed someone to cross the distance of my need.

And the angel came to Elijah a second time and said for him to get up and eat and added a special statement, "The journey is too hard for you." So Elijah ate the cake and drank the water and felt so much better he traveled for forty days and forty nights on the strengthening of God's care.

I'm a theater person, and I see the next scene with staging and lighting and a full set. It's a cave, a dark cave, and Elijah spends the night there. And God Almighty calls to him:

The following is scripted to enhance the dramatic value of the story's theatricality.

GREAT GOD ALMIGHTY: *(speaking from outside the cave)* What are you doing here?

ELIJAH: *(speaking from inside the cave)* It's just like I've been telling you, Most Holy God. I've worked my heart out for you, Most Holy God. I've told people they were sinners and you, Most Holy God, know where they live and their cell phone numbers. I told them to stop sitting on the fence shrugging their shoulders and murmuring "Whatever" to each other.

GREAT GOD ALMIGHTY: I appreciate that. You've done well. I am not fond of the expression "Whatever." I wrote a few words about it—expressing my attitude and reaction toward those who are neither hot nor cold. It's in the back of my Book, but most readers don't get that far. Now, as to what you were saying—

ELIJAH: I've risked losing my life, my job, and my special parking space—

GREAT GOD ALMIGHTY: You have shown great courage.

ELIJAH: And I won for you, Most Holy God. And you, Most Holy God, brought down fire and rain, and it was wonderful—wonderful—up there on the mountaintop. I could feel your power like a winner's wreath of fresh laurel holding my body in your holy embrace, but it didn't change the hearts of the people. Oh Most Holy God, the children of Israel have turned away from your law, torn down your altars, and killed your prophets. I am all you've got left, and things don't look too good for me either.

GREAT GOD ALMIGHTY: Go out and stand on the mountain before the Lord.

ELIJAH: OK.

And when Elijah steps outside, the Lord passes by, and the stage effects outdo themselves. A mighty wind moves the backdrop of painted mountains. Rocks and stones and pieces of branches shower the stage. There is the sound of wind and earthquake and the zipping and zapping of laser beams and throbbing of fluorescent lights, and you in the audience sense what Elijah felt. The power of Almighty God in earthquake and fire, and in them all is the silence of God.

49

Because even Elijah, God's chosen prophet who had exhausted himself in obedience to God, even Elijah had to hear the new voice of God. God in his absolute sovereignty. Not the voice of the people, not the voice of the enemy, not the voice of wind and earthquakes, but silence. Silence in which the quiet whisperings of God would speak loudly of his authority.

God told Elijah that he would accept his resignation, but he was not closing the office. He had work to be done, through that very office, and some of it was Elijah's assignment. He told Elijah to get up and get back to work, to anoint kings and his successor Elisha. And then God set the record straight. He told Elijah that there were many believers (seven thousand) in Israel who had not and would not bow down to Baal, the chief of the pagan gods.

God told Elijah all of that. And Elijah heard him. In Hebrew the word for *hear* implies obedience. To hear the Word of the Lord is to obey the Word of the Lord. Elijah heard God and obeyed him and served him and proved himself to be a man of God. I doubt that Elijah was ever anything less than a willing prophet, but I do know that sometimes when God is silent, it is because a disobedient heart has a deaf ear. God often uses winds and fires and earthquakes of the soul to clear our ears of old authorities, self-authorized leadership, and the clogging cluttering of false gods, that we might hear and obey the still voice of God.

And Elijah obeyed.

Elijah was a great man of God, a mighty prophet who dared to stand for the one God when he, Elijah, thought there weren't any others.

Believing the job can't be done is the second worst reason for quitting. The first is believing that God cannot do in you and in me what he purposed. That reasoning delays our action of obedience and sets us on the path of defeat. In it we think God is silent, but he is just waiting to give the cue for the wind and the rain and the display of his power.

In the silence of God, hold to three words. Say them over and over to yourself. Write them on your daily calendar; share them with a friend. They are like the cake and water that the angels brought or the cookies from my neighbor. Three words: God is able. In the lightning, in the fire, in the earthquake, in the rain—and most especially in the silence—God is able!

CHAPTER 6

Tick Tock

What do the following have in common?

A lawyer presenting his final statement to the jury

A farmer planting his crops

A surprise birthday party

A heart transplant

A builder directing the pouring of concrete

A young man proposing to his sweetheart

The announcement of the merger of two giant companies

A successful manicure

A night club comedienne

A tightrope artist

Lance Armstrong

A parent telling a child about the wonders of sex
A space liftoff
Just about everything you can think of

What do they have in common? Timing. Timing is the essence of success in any venture.

In the silences of God, I deeply appreciate the concerned attention of anyone who cares, and it always helps. However, I have found that some of the words that are supposed to bring me out of the darkness and into the light don't.

I am told to trust in God! Right! I hand out that advice without any hesitation, no matter what the situation of need. I have questions about trusting God. What do I trust God to do? Solve my problems as I present to him my requests? Good idea, but he doesn't always do that. In fact, at this stage of my life, I am often as grateful for the times he did not agree with my solutions as for the times he did. As a child I prayed that God would allow me to be a high-wire artist in the circus; I did not know then that I am afraid of heights. God may have placed me in a circus, but at least my high wire is on low ground. Trust God for what? *Trust God to be God.* Trust God to be sovereign. Trust God to do the right thing. Trust God to listen and consider your request. Trust God's faithfulness, his love, his wisdom, and trust his sovereign timing. He is infallible in the matter of timing.

Take, for instance, the story of Ruth. This little book in the Old Testament is a tale of romance, adventure, and the never failing timing of God.

Once upon a time, a long time ago, there was a young woman whose name was Delight. Because of a famine in their land, Judah, Delight and her husband moved to Moab with their two sons.

The two sons married two girls who were pretty, proper, and pagan. Delight's sons and her husband died, which meant she was in a foreign land under a foreign god and had no job, future, or health insurance; and since she was a woman and a foreigner, she had no voice in changing any of the circumstances. She heard the famine in Judah was over, so she decided to move back to her home. Moving back home meant packing the little that she owned in a tote bag and heading out to walk the distance to Bethlehem in Judah—and to walk it alone. However, as she was going out of the city gate, she looked back, and there were her two daughters-in-law following her like two puppies smelling out a roast beef sandwich. They told Delight they were going with her. She put down her tote bag and told them to stay put in Moab where they could find husbands, which Delight was in no condition to give them. One of the daughters, Orpah, decided to go back to Moab. The other daughter, named Ruth, said she had no intention of going back but was going with Delight, and as she put it, "Your people shall be my people and your God, my God."

Ruth's statement deserves special consideration. Ruth was making a major change. She was changing lands, she was changing cultures, and she was changing sovereign allegiance. She converted to Jehovah God. Right there at the gate of Moab, Ruth was turning her life over to the God of Abraham, Isaac, and Jacob. This is amazing! How did Ruth know about Jehovah God? She heard about him from her mother-in-law. Her mother-in-law was so depressed that she changed her name from Naomi, which means "delight," to Mara which means "bitterness."

Depression didn't keep Delight, now Mara, from talking about Jehovah, whose name never changed. Mara, that tired and weary woman from Judah, was enclosed in the silence of God, but she never stopped talking about him. She believed life was grim but Jehovah was great. She believed that sorrow was a way of life but God was a way of hope. Depression may break your heart, but it need not silence your testimony. Somewhere in the silence of God, there in the misery of Moab, this woman from Bethlehem shared enough of her faith to convert her daughter-in-law.

Depression has its own style of silence. The walls of depression often are lined with mirrors, and all we see is ourselves. The doors of depression are soundproofed so the only voices we hear are our own. Enclosed in depression, we doubt there is anything but misery, unfairness, pain, and the encompassing of God's silence. I know depression. I have been in its soggy grip and know its despair. Don't mock the depressed with empty phrases, but don't abandon them to their darkness. It may be they can't get out, but God can get in.

There are many styles and types of depression, and there are many styles and types of treatment. Surprisingly enough, most of them work. The odds for recovery from depression are high. The odds for believing that, when you are depressed, are very low. The depressed are not always helped when told how fortunate they are because that adds guilt. And depression absorbs guilt and packs it away for the midnights of the soul. Depression is not always lessened when told that your great aunt had it for fifty years and then got strangled in a garden vine because she thought she was a strawberry. It is good for the depressed to have the kind of help that names its causative and knows enough to know how to help and to know when what is known doesn't help. Sometimes depression is a result of weariness, and doing nothing but rest is a great idea, but depression can celebrate activity. You can attend a Bible class even when you're depressed. It is not generally known, but you can teach a Bible class when you're depressed. I know because I have done it. You can talk about the Lord when you're depressed. Many of the psalms of King David ring with testimony to the Lord during depression. Read them while you weep; they will give your silent hurting a language with words to release its sorrow.

I think Naomi, which means "delight," spoke words about Jehovah while she was depressed and called herself Mara, which means "bitterness." And at least one daughter-in-law, Ruth, heard her and claimed her faith.

Naomi, now called Bitterness, picked up her tote bag and went to Bethlehem with Ruth, now called Believer. In Bethlehem they found a celebration going on because everyone was involved in the barley harvest. They also found Boaz who, right off the bat, found Ruth, and romance blossomed in the barley fields. Boaz and Ruth were married, Mara went back to being Naomi, and in the proper length of time had an even better name—Grandma! That baby was named Obed. Obed became the father of Jesse, and Jesse became the father of David the king, whose psalms of praise flourished in depression. What a neat story. And none of it would have happened were it not for God's perfect and detailed timing.

All the wonder of the book of Ruth and the romance and the lineage unto David, Israel's king, depended on the timing of God. Ruth and her mother-in-law arrived at Bethlehem at the time of the barley harvest. At no other time would the story have unfolded.

In the season of sorrow and silence, in the awkward quiet of depression, trust God. Trust his perfect timing. It is in effect in your deepest sorrow; it is in effect in your highest joy.

After a rehearsal I drove home but thought of something I needed at the grocery store and drove back to get it. As I got to my doorway, I thought of something I needed at the drugstore and left my house to go get it. Coming back home, I drove a couple of turns around a circle near my house and then into my driveway. As I pulled up to my back door, I saw the lights of a car coming into my driveway. Having been warned by news reports of hurtful happenings, I was cautious and looked carefully at the driver of the car approaching me. It was Dr. Jim Moore and his wife, June. They are dear friends. Dr. Moore's church, Houston's St. Luke's United Methodist, houses the children's theater of the A.D. Players. June and Jim had driven by to leave me a note when they saw my car pulling into the driveway. We had a wonderful visit, exchanging prayer requests and sharing in the rare privilege of fellowship. As we were talking, still standing in my driveway, I suddenly asked Jim, "How did he do that? How did God Almighty, at full-time work keeping the stars in place, get the three of us together?" Twice I had come to my back door and turned away. Twice I had gone around the circle near my house. If I had come five minutes later, I would have missed them. If they had come five minutes earlier, they would have missed me. The sovereign timing of God—down to the minute.

At that moment the precious visit with June and Jim came just in the nick of time. I learned God was in the minute. When I see him in the minute, I can trust him for the hour. When I know him in the hour, I can trust him for the day. When his lordship decorates my day, I can trust him in the month; and when I can trust him in the month, the year is his.

In the silences of God, trust in the timing of God. His clock may not be set by your watch, but your watch will keep better time when it's set to his clock.

Memo

At the start of the day, I mentioned to God that time was too short for sufficient sleeping hours and politely reminded my Most Holy God that this was an untimely time for one assistant to be on vacation and another ill. I assured God he was in control but there were some details for which my view was apparently better than his and he was not giving those details his full attention. At my office I buried my face in my hands and prayed prayers that defined errors under God's wayward directions, disaffecting the post office system and allowing correspondence to miss a few critical beats.

Having lunch brought in because of the little time problem God seemed to be having, I commented negatively on avocados, brimming with health and energy and beauty, and also full of fat calories, nothing more than well-packaged butter—obviously some error in God's ecological system.

I continued helpful hints unto the Most High God from my desk, which, due to God's miscalculation, was so crowded with papers and out-of-date calendars that I could not find the listing of matters relevant to the telephone interview that had already been postponed three times because of that recurrent problem with God's timing.

The day limped through its hours, and I left my office for home just in time to catch my breath at the sight of the sunset. Ripples of colors, patterns of time dancing with itself. "Beautiful," I whispered, and God said, "Jeannette, I'm so glad you like something I have done. Maybe the sunset might give me good favor." And I wept.

Oh, God, your ways are perfect, and you have no problem with time. Thank you for being patient when I do.

CHAPTER 7

It's Your Cue

*T*he silences of God are real. In the first place he has every right to his pauses. He is God. He can speak when and if he chooses.

Allow God his mysteries.

Often we pester him for answers like petulant children whining for the why of his direction. In his sovereign wisdom, his choices of silence are the right answers whether we find that comfortable or not. Countless times his answer to me has been full and rich and enough—but not to my demanding ears.

In a recent quandary I held God accountable to his promises of answering. I shared with him a long-winded phrasing of philosophical questioning. Hearing nothing, I turned to the Scriptures for comfort, or perhaps a godly apology, and found Psalm 46:10. Clearly I got my answer: "Hush, and know that

I am God." The being of God—past the answers. The essence of God—past my questions.

It is at times a harsh principle, but God will not dispense answers upon demand. He is bigger and wiser than that. He is not a divine fortune cookie. He is not straw in the wind. He is God, and his silence may be our holiest answer.

God does not give us too much information. Many years ago I thought that if I started a Bible class, God would, of course, supply a teacher. I invited a few of my theater friends to drop by my house on one afternoon for coffee and cookies and mumbled something to them about bringing a Bible. They agreed to attend with some reluctance, and I was confident that God would arrange to have a teacher for us. Two days before the class, I realized I was to be the teacher. I was terrified. I said to God, "Dear Lord, you have never made a mistake, but now you are so close to error that I'm scared."

I went to a Bible bookstore and asked for a commentary. The clerk asked for what age, meaning spiritual capacity, and I answered "mature," not meaning spiritual capacity. I bought a large brown-leathered commentary that I don't yet understand. After the first few pages I considered canceling the class and was hesitant about even opening the Bible again. I had more information than I was able to tabulate.

God always hands out his wisdom with careful consideration of our capacity to practice what he preaches. We may need to keep the information on a back shelf while we learn enough to appropriate it. The great artist Rembrandt once said to a questioning student, "Put into practice what you now know, and in time you will have the answers you seek." The silence of God often gives us time to mull over what he's already said. Revelation is a processed understanding. God may move quickly in the distribution, but he gets us through the order as specifically as A to B to C. I keep asking for T before I've really gotten hold of D, and God waits for me to sit up, shut up, and catch up.

Celebrate his silences. He may be silently inviting us into the ease of companionable silence in this noise-oriented generation. And then with all the offering and giving and receiving and waiting, God may be silent to get us to listen, or he may be silent to get us to speak. To speak words of confession, words of remorse, words of gratitude, words of acceptance, words of joy, words of praise, words of fellowship, words of obedience, and—most specifically—words of needs articulated.

"Don't worry about anything, but in everything . . . let your requests be made known to God" (Phil. 4:6). I debated with that verse. Why should I make my requests known to God? Being God, he knows them already.

We are to articulate our requests for four reasons:

1. He said so! And that's reason enough.
2. We need to know we've said them so we can know God listens and answers.
3. We need to make our requests known to God not because he needs to hear them but because we need to say them.
4. All needs, both good and bad, get better when they are articulated.

Dear God,
I would tell you my needs, but I can't define them. They are entombed in
the bubble wrap of hurts. They travel along with me in safety, but I can't
identify them in their swollen wrappings. And dear God, I am afraid they
are so trivial that even if I could identify them, they should never be in
your presence. Some of them are old, but they have been revived with fresh
tears, and I am embarrassed to find them still running wild like barefooted
children while the rest of me is growing older. Some are as fresh as this
morning, and I can't bear to look at them. I'll pack them away until
I forget their damage, but then there is your Word of insistence. So I'll tell
you my need. I will come as you requested, with words—words jumbled
and out of order like a Scrabble board's tiles spilled into a sack. Words
dusty from the attic where I hid them. Words I do not understand because
I don't really know how what happened happened. Words, words, words.
And here is my need expressed: Dear Lord, I need my needs clarified that
I may articulate them.

I want the angry people to like me again and those who thought me
sweet and kind to forgive me for the times I'm not. I want to be true to
you and to let others see you in me without explaining how someone with
good intentions finds herself blocking the view. I want to get my hair cut
and lose fifteen pounds almost immediately. I want to have already read
that weighty book that someone gave me, saying it was just what I needed
and I don't understand it. And I want to have back the time I wasted by
not articulating my needs because now that I know them I'm running
short on time to tell them, but I'll be back a little later, and along the way
I'll mention those I missed. Oh, and one more thing, Lord, thank you for
listening.
Amen.

Philippians 4:6 means what it says, "Let your requests be made known to God." I honestly have requests made known unto God that I would not admit to anyone else. He may not answer them as I suggest, but he will listen and consider; and even if he does not answer my request, he will answer me. And that was what I most needed in the first place.

Mary Crowley told of an experience she had that forever underlined her intention to make her needs known to God. Mary was to be honored at the naming of a building for her in downtown Dallas. Preparing for that event, Mary had ordered a dress designed and made in Paris; had been to a week of revitalizing at a spa; was primped, pampered, and poised for the celebration. She got into her car, beautifully dressed in a full-length fur coat and matching hat. It was a stormy night, so Mary left a little early to arrive on time. She said that she was praising God as she drove into downtown Dallas, until she looked at her gas gauge. It was steady on E. She began to peer through the rain for the sign of a filling station and realized there were none between where she was and the building to be named for her. With her eyes open, she prayed as she drove, "Dear Lord, I thank you for this honor, and I will use it to bring praise to your name. However, I am out of gas, and there is no filling station in this part of Dallas. Please God, I need a filling station." Mary said she drove up a small hill leading into downtown Dallas as her car began sputtering in its emptiness. Through the rain pelting her windshield, Mary saw a filling station. She has said she never saw it before and never saw it afterward, but there it was—provided by God. Praising the Lord, she coasted down the hill and into the station. It was a self-service station.

Mary Crowley, in her Paris dress, fur coat, fur hat, and full hairdo, in the driving rain, pumped gas before receiving her honors. She said she raised her hand through the torrent of rain-drops and said, "Lord, never again will I fail to be specific."

In the silence of God, let your requests be made known, and be specific.

In theater, we actors work with what we call "actions," motivations or intentions. Artistic energy is found in specifying to ourselves what we want to do. There may be long intentions, far-seeing intentions, ultimate desires that plot the progress of our course; but often we need to modify that ultimate purpose with short intentions that can be immediately realized. In the silence of God, we Christians gain balance by expressing agree-ment with God's ultimate intentions. "God, if this is to your purpose and glory, I am content in it." That point of view is right, honoring to God, and satisfying to us.

Frequently, as a director, I will say to an actor, "Find a more immediate intention. Play the scene with short distance motivations." Such changes often afford energy and a person-alizing of the event. In the silence of God, I also find those "short" intentions to be helpful. I can't visualize the outcome. The end result, in the hands of God, is beyond the immediacy of my needs in crisis. I find action needful in the lethargy of being overwhelmed, and then I call upon shorter goals. In the dilemma of God's mysterious silence, within the overreaching of a long-term goal, address the underreaching of immediacy. Focus on small purposes and do the next good thing. Direct your action to short-term intentions you can meet. It may be so immediate as calling a friend, writing a note, doing what you do—washing the dishes, alphabetically counting blessings, little good things that give light to the darkness of despair. When the big needs are beyond words, express the little needs that fit your condition. Dare to look your needs in the face and share them in the face of God. One outstanding demand in this exercise is to be honest with God. He may be the only one who can handle your honesty.

Sometimes in the silence of God is our anger—anger that has never been expressed and, therefore, has not had benefit of healing. If it is anger with God, it needs to be addressed and confessed because if repressed, it will lock you in separating silence.

I often look at the story of God's prophet Jonah. I understand him. I have not the grandeur of his mission or the obvious power of his words, but I understand his personal dilemma. Jonah did what God didn't want him to do, and it turned out to be a whale of a problem. Then Jonah did what he didn't want to do, and Jonah became the problem.

In the first place, what about that whale? God will go to any lengths to get his prophet back in working order. In the whale's belly, in the comings and goings of whale food all about him, Jonah caught on to what fellowship with God is all about. Out of the whale Jonah was still in deep water. He plopped down on the shores of Nineveh, which was exactly where he didn't want to be in the first place.

Now Jonah had the vengeance of God as the wind beneath his sails, and he ran all over Nineveh telling the people their time was up, God had had it, and they were doomed, damned, and dismissed. What a sermon! No need for a closing verse or the announcement of the next church supper.

No sooner had the words come from Jonah's screaming throat than the people of Nineveh repented. Down on their knees, praying to God for forgiveness. And then, right in front of Jonah, who hadn't yet washed the whale oil out of his hair, right in front of this angry preacher, God Almighty forgave Nineveh. That made Jonah furious. The only fun he had in his mission was thinking about Nineveh sweating it out in hell, and there was God putting out the welcome mat to heaven. "That is not fair," Jonah said, and settled himself under a gourd tree on a hillside with his cap over his eyes, his hands over his ears, and a pout on his face that God could read from a distance. And now it wasn't Nineveh or the whale that was the problem; it was Jonah. Then God asked Jonah one of the most arresting questions on record, "Is it right for you to be angry?" (Jonah 4:4).

Anger is a major block to a vital dialogue with God. It's almost impossible to chitchat with this sovereign God of grace and love and at the same time be locked in a monologue with anger. What God did on a cross in the body of his Son, Jesus the Christ, tore open the veil in the temple. That same power opens the locked shutters of our anger when we hear God's question, "Is your anger reasonable?" It was an honest question and is just as clarifying now as it was for Jonah.

Anger is a haughty tyrant, and one of its demands is self-imposed loneliness—a legislated solitude that locks the door against fellowship. There is no brotherhood and sisterhood in bitterness, for even those who agree with you are brought together by the strength of the argument, not its resolution.

Any bondage of argument requires the consistent reinforcement of the hurtful issue, or the bondage is broken. The members of the offended brotherhood have to keep reminding one another of its pain, and no member can dare to heal. That is a shaky fellowship at best and at its worst is a commitment to misery.

Look at your anger. Give it words. Is it reasonable? Discuss it with God. He may be the only one who can handle it. You can't, your friends can't, your coworkers can't, your ministry can't, your celebrations can't—and I don't even think the whale could. That's why under God's command the whale was just as eager to get rid of Jonah as Jonah was to get out of the whale.

Look at your anger. In the light of what God has done for you, are you still locked away from him because of what he didn't do that you wanted done? Or maybe it was what God did that you didn't want done. Did you try to be God and fail so badly that your ministry became a mockery? Did you, on your saintly pilgrimage, trip over the hem of your humanity and fall facedown in the garbage of rotting intentions?

Is your anger reasonable? That's what God asked Jonah, and I think he asks modifications of that question even today. Settle down with God for a reasonable discussion. Have a chat with the sovereign leader over a couple of cups of coffee. He won't drink his, and you won't want yours, but the fixing of it will give you something to do until the talking starts.

In the silence talk to God. Bring him words. He asked for them. If your anger is reasonable, turn its retribution over to him. If it's unreasonable—and usually face-to-face with God, mine is—if it's unreasonable, give it up. Why should an unreasonable cause keep you and me from the God of unreasonable grace?

In the silence of God, it may well be that it's time for you and for me to start talking. There might be an awful lot of ground to cover with words, but I have found that once I start the talking, the conversation moves right along. God is a good listener. And his listening breaks the silence.

Dear Lord,

I am not a preacher or a scholar; I am an actress and a director. And part of my job is to know and to be able to convey feelings. This morning I saw an angry face. It was reflected in my mirror. Makeup couldn't cover it, a made-up smile couldn't lighten it, and I recognized in the tightening of the mouth and the slanting of the eyes and the puffiness of hurts packed deep, that the mirrored face was that of an angry person.

Lord, I really like being happy. I have a friend who doesn't. She's happier when she's unhappy, but I would rather be happy, and people like me better when I'm happy. In fact, I'm afraid I have to be happy for people to like me at all. I would like to come into your presence, but I see unhappiness in my face, and I'm afraid for you to see that too.

The mirror is right. I'm angry, God. What was done to me was not right! And if it had been done to someone else, it would not be right! I don't seek vengeance. I don't want that enormous responsibility. I don't demand the wrong be corrected; that is in your hands, Most Sovereign God. I just want my feelings authenticated and to face you with my anger because I can't handle it.

Thank you, Lord. Your love didn't blink an eye. That face in my mirror looks a whole lot better. Anger rules over self-imposed loneliness,

and your fellowship just walked through the door of my tear-locked heart.
Amen.
Oh, P.S. Lord, While you're here, could you help me with the makeup?
There are some mirror images Mary Kay can't help.

CHAPTER 8

Baggage Tags

Soon after I was married, I was speaking at a conference in Tyler. There had been all sorts of dignitaries there, and several of them had flown in on private planes or on flights rerouted. My flights in and out were as regularly scheduled, and my hosts arranged for me to be taken directly to the airport after my closing presentation. I assured them they need not stay with me as I had only a short time to wait for my plane, and I graciously sent them on their way. Assuming my flight would be as planned, I would easily make my connection and be back at home with my husband, who was meeting my plane and going with me to a program in Houston later that evening. It was not only early in my marriage but early in my traveling, and I thought everything would go as scheduled. It did not.

The rerouting of the airline schedule and the increased activity of private planes had disaffected the quiet of the Tyler airport. The baggage handlers were handling rescheduled travelers, my flight was cancelled, and the one replacing it would not make my change of planes in Dallas. As traveling was a fairly new adventure to me, I was no longer the poised and gracious lady who had been on the speaker's platform but much like a distraught chicken ruffled by two storms attacking her feathers from opposite directions.

I did not have change for the telephone and borrowed a coin from the ticket counter and called home. I requested the charges be met by the receiver, and my husband's voice was pleasant and calm, which I received as a butter pecan ice cream cone on a hot day. The operator asked for my name, and I said, "Jeannette Clift," and my name was relayed to my husband who paused and then said, "What is the name again, please?" The operator repeated my name louder and clearer, and my husband said, as though struggling to remember, "Jeannette Clift, Jeannette Clift, you say?" I yelled into the telephone, "No, operator, I am Jeannette Clift George." Everyone in the airport heard me, and so did my husband. Not even bothering to disguise his laughter, he said, "Of course, operator, I am pleased to receive a call from Jeannette Clift George." I hasten to explain that my husband never was in any way threatened or uncomfortable with my professional name. He was enjoying the joke and also managed to arrange the changes needed for the evening's program. However, I did hear a principle: in reversing the charges, it is wise to know exactly who you are!

In the silence of God, affirm your identity and your relationship, and in a constantly changing world be assured that some things never change. My personal identity was preset before I was married. However, the system of charges reversed depended on whose I was in order to serve who I was. I was my husband's wife, and on that basis who I was had every right to reverse the charges!

Colossians 2 announces a miraculous change that has occurred in the believer. It is said of God, in verse 13, that he has delivered us out from under the power of darkness. That deliverance can be trusted to hold true just as surely in the silence of God as in his times of frequent personal communication.

If you have never known a time when God was silent, don't be bothered. You are no less loved than those hurting in the absence of God whispering or thundering in their ears. However, if you continue reading, you will gain principles that will give you compassion for those who do know the experience. You don't have to fall into a ditch to help your fallen neighbor, but knowing the experience does hasten your assistance.

In Colossians we are told that the believer has been taken out from under the power, the authority, of evil. That's great! Disconnected from a negative power and surely set free. But that freedom doesn't really get us where we're going. We're out but not in. God's deliverance is full. He got the whole job done. Out from under, we were brought into fellowship. The kingdom of his Son. The believer has been brought out from under the negative authority and brought into a close personal relationship with God himself through his Son.

My husband loved me. I loved him. In that love we made a commitment of relationship. The telephone call did not begin the relationship; it merely actuated what had already been established.

As a Christian, when hurting in the silence of God, I am seeking activation of a relationship that has not been broken even by the silence. I need to know that in order to make my telephone call with the charges reversed. That unbroken relationship is what the verses in Colossians are all about. Redemption. Forgiveness. I need to keep my mind alert to those truths that do not change because the circumstances of my life change a lot. In that Tyler airport, schedules changed, the baggage handler changed, and I didn't have the change to make the call and had to borrow it. In the silence of God, reaffirm what will not change.

Colossians also gives us two principles that we can cling to in the silence of God. The letter of Colossians was written to a people philosophically bewildered. Many of the messages we receive today are bewildering. The other night I was watching television, and I didn't even understand the commercials. I watched two of them and didn't catch on to what they were selling. It may be generational, but I have to look carefully to find the funny of today's funny papers. (I love the funny papers and believe we adults need them far more than the children. I'm happy to recommend several comic strips that I earnestly believe are more essential to a good morning than that first cup of coffee.)

At my age I can remember a time when funny papers were all funny, we women all wore hats and gloves, and we all *watched* radio. We sat in a semicircle and watched a great big radio without taking our eyes off of it. I remember as a little girl visiting my aunt who had a big lavish house with a special sitting room for the radio, and the chairs were all positioned so the family and the guests could all *watch* it! We talked out of the sides of our mouths so we wouldn't miss any of it. I saw good shows on radio.

As for now, I find we are subject to many confusing messages from all communicating agencies. That was the problem being addressed by the letter to the Colossians. In the midst of confusing, convoluting, and contradicting philosophies, a strategic and critical statement was being made about Jesus! Colossians 2:9 says clearly that in the person of Jesus the Christ all the fullness of God, the Godhead, was comfortably at home. That is as controversial today as it was then. People were dying for it then, and people are dying for it today, and people like me are living by it. It is his identity that secures mine and his plan that includes me as an active participant.

One of God's choicest gifts is the opportunity for participation in his great work. Paul the apostle thanked the little church at Philippi for their fellowship in the work, their participation in his ministry, and their active partnership in the distribution of the good news. That gift of active involvement comes with the name tag of identity in the family of the living God. Christianity is not just an event for the grandstand. It is a call to the players. And God has made an awesome promise to his team: he will not leave us out of the action.

Corrie ten Boom was one of the most totally productive people I have ever known. She was resolute in her intentions to serve, to speak, to proclaim. The accented voice of that little

Dutch lady was actually heard around the world and always announcing that Jesus is victor. In her last illness, she was quiet, frail, mute. But God had made a promise to her, and God keeps all his promises. From her silent bed she prayed for those with whom she had worked, for those whom she had known in her extensive travels, and for those whose activity was on the field she could no longer serve. I am one of those for whom she prayed, and she was and ever will be a participant in my life.

That is included in God's gift of life, the opportunity of service. I believe each believer is equipped to participate in the gospel. I am not left out, and neither are you. Regardless of the circumstances we have daily the choice of participating.

There are times in the silences of God when we incorrectly assume we are left out, not counted in, of no value to God or to man or to the postman or the singles' banquet or the women's fellowship or the men's Bible class. In the silence we feel we are no longer of the in-bunch.

Idleness can be a premium time of rest. It also can be a devastating time of personal loss—loss of involvement, loss of importance, loss of significance, and loss of communication. I hurriedly run to the rescue with a reminder: God makes the insignificant significant, not the assignment. Assignments change. God does not. He does not tease us with his gifts or leave us when they change. In this day he offers us the option of participation.

That option is based on the surety of who Jesus is. God in him and he in me, an active fellowship between the believer and the never-ending story of God. In the silence of God, what he has given us has a voice of its own. Hear it again in Colossians:

all the fullness of the Godhead is comfortably at home in him. Now what does that mean that is valid for all times? What does the proclaimed deity of Christ have to do with me? Merely everything. According to the Scripture—which I believe, according to what God has already said—which I can believe even when he's silent—the fullness of Jesus who is the Christ means that *I am complete* in him. I am complete. I am a whole being.

Someone gave me an orchid. I'm not good with plants, so I've asked for help with this one. And now it is a stately white flower on a slender stem that is about two feet tall. It's gorgeous! That flower was once inside a little tiny seed. Everything but the green bow was in that seed complete. I'm going to follow the directions about my orchid. I'll water it and give it the care the attached card tells me to follow, but the orchid was complete in the seed. I am complete in Jesus Christ. I am a complete me. I'm not perfect, and God has quite a bit more to do with me, but I am complete because Jesus is.

When my husband accepted my telephone call, he didn't accept it because I was perfect—although he has at times thought that I was. He did not even accept it because I had just spoken for a high-style conference that had governors and dignitaries flying in on their private planes. He didn't accept it because I had money; I had to borrow the coin to make the call. He accepted it because I was me, his wife.

In the silence of God, remember what you know is true and will not change. Celebrate who Jesus is. Identify yourself, to you and to the problem, whom you know yourself to be in Christ. And then participate in the gospel with joy.

Now what in the world does this have to do with the problem of God's silences and how to survive in them?

1. Reacquaint yourself with what you know is true and will not change.
2. Celebrate who Jesus is.
3. Identify yourself as whom you know yourself to be in him.
4. Enjoy the connection.

Short Script with Long Principle

Hello, operator. I'd like to make a call please. It's to God. That's right. God Almighty. Well, you see, I haven't heard from him today, and I wanted to be sure I'm all right. I know he's all right. He's God. Anyway, it's a collect call, and you'll see in your records that he's already paid the charges. Tell him it's Jeannette calling. He knows me. He gets a lot of calls from me, and he always answers. Well, you see, the day started out a little bumpy. I had to work late last night, and this morning I had to get up early. My first meeting was even earlier than when I got there, and I kept running all day just trying to catch up, and I've not made it. I didn't plan on looking this way either; it just happened and—you've got him? A direct line? That's neat. Tell him it's Jeannette. Oh Lord, I forgot that I have a direct line. Thank you.

CHAPTER 9

Well Done

I had made a tight connection in Atlanta and was a little breathless when I boarded the plane. The flight looked full as I glanced back at the seated passengers. I don't know why the passengers who have already boarded always look at latecomers as though the latecomers had really not been invited. I usually look like I wasn't sure I was invited and am hoping to sneak in on someone else's invitation. And then to get to my seat, I have to walk through the first-class passengers who are already being served drinks. They make me feel that the only place for me is out on a wing.

I am pleased when I get upgraded to first class, even though I spend most of the flight telling the flight attendants and the fellow passengers that I don't usually fly first class. I'm a Christian and am not supposed to be comfortable, I explain to people who really don't care and just hope I'm not going to talk like that throughout the flight.

On one flight when I was in first class, I was hoping to get some needed work done. I had just opened my notebook when a gentleman boarded late and hurried to the seat beside me. He had started talking, and loud, before he got seated. He told me about his brother's wife who had taken him to the plane and wore sandals that kept slipping off as she drove. He thought they shouldn't allow women drivers to wear sandals like that, but their son was going to be a splendid ball player! I nodded every time he took a breath, which wasn't often, and went back to my notebook, but it didn't even slow him down. He told me he had gone to school with the governor of Arkansas and was on his way to get a contract signed by a representative of a company in Cuba.

Everything he said had an exclamation point after it, and I think he thought my notebook was to take down what he said, so he repeated some of the words louder. Then, settled in place and ready for a long visit, he said, "Now tell me, little lady, what do you do?"

I looked him straight in the eye and said, "I'm a fund-raiser." I have no idea why I said that. I've never said it before, and although I am the artistic director of a company always happy to be supported, I would never call myself a fund-raiser. I said it though, without blinking an eye: "I am a fund-raiser." He never said another word to me. He turned away from me, put the radio plugs in his ear, and went to sleep. I got my study finished, and the flight attendant was so tickled she gave me a dollar donation for my company. I claimed an identity that was not false but did not accurately reflect my work.

The flight from Atlanta's connection was a different plane, and I was seated in the back. I was glad to have an aisle seat and stowed my carry-on quickly and sat down. The couple beside me smiled. She sat at the window and he in the middle seat beside me.

We exchanged hello pleasantries, and after we took off we settled back in our seats, enjoying our snacks. I was delighted by the pretzels, which were a welcome relief from peanuts. There was once an airline that served chili! Good chili with crisp cheese crackers, but they went out of business. I guess the chili cost so much more than peanuts that the little airline couldn't make it.

The lady by the window said to her husband, "Ask her what she does." He did, and I said, "I'm in theater," and he told his wife, "She's in theater." The lady thought that was exciting and told him to ask me if I had done any movies. I said yes, I had, and he told her. She thought that was wonderful and asked him to ask me what movies. I said I had done several but only one had been generally distributed. He told his wife, "She has done a lot of movies, but only one has been successful." His wife was sympathetic to that news and told her husband to ask me which one was successful. I said, *The Hiding Place,* and he told her *The Hiding Place,* and she nearly flipped out of the plane. *The Hiding Place,* she said. "We had that at our church. It was wonderful. Ask her what part she played." He said, "What part did you play?" and I said "Corrie," and he told his wife that

I played the part of Corrie. She leaned over him, turned her head to look at me, and then settled back in her chair saying, "Not the night we saw it!"

It's a movie, I thought. It has the same cast every night. And then I began to wonder. Could they have taken me out? No, I had to be in it because I did it. I don't think I ever convinced the lady, but I have laughed at the memory of our conversation.

In the silence of God, what is not so funny is the trickery by which we are tempted to lose our respect for ourselves and our regard for the work of God through us. The questions are, Who am I, and what do I do? Knowing that is finding personal security even in the silence of God. I am deeply aware that the hand of God accomplishes through me his good purposes. It is his sovereignty, his produce, and we are but gloves on his hands, the pursuers of his will and the occupants of his grace. However, there is also the privilege of personal accountability to his call. Faith is energy. It is not the conclusion but the conduit to his work. It is the energy that activates our behavior that we may do our work well, unto His glory and our processed satisfaction. Good work is good work and needs to be heralded by the worker as well as those who receive it.

Believer, find joy in your work! The Bible says he gives us generously all things to enjoy. One of the resources of joy is work well done and, sadly enough, we Christians are frequently so afraid our humility is marginal that we fail to claim personal involvement.

I well remember one time when a gentle lady came up after I had done a program in her church, and with the kindest of smiles she told me I had done well and that she appreciated my talk. Bless her heart, by the time I finished telling her that I had done nothing but God had done everything and I deserved no credit of compliment, she went away feeling strangely rebuked, and I went away shining with my self-applied humility. I watched the lady as she went to her car, and something about the drooping shoulders made me reexamine my response to her kindness. I was aware of God reminding me of a significant fact, "Jeannette, if you had listened carefully, you would have understood she did not say you had created the world. She merely said she liked your talk."

My favorite parable is a little one in the Gospel of Mark. Jesus tells about a man who planted seed and went to sleep by night and rose by day, and the seed sprouted and grew, and the man didn't have the vaguest notion how it did that, but in time the harvest came. I love that. It is a sermon in a second: man did his work, and God did his work, and they celebrated the harvest as a natural processing of man's work and God's mystery.

In the silence of God, don't let the wily enemy who knows exactly when we are the most vulnerable take away the fact of your good work. The produce is God's; the work itself is a privileged gift from him. But when your back aches from too much bending and planting and your hands are cut from the scratching of pods and leaves and your eyes are weary from seeking the sun for its seasons, don't let God's silence make you think your work was for nothing. You, child of God, are in the work under God.

Weariness is worsened when the work is considered wasted. Long before the harvest, long before the first sprouting seed, long before the garnishing of rewards, God smiles on the worker and says, "My child, your work is good." And once in a while in, of course, a proper attitude, we should agree, because it's just not smart to disagree with God.

A Short Tail with a Hoppy Ending

Oscar Overstep was a rabbit. Not a little fluffy, pink-eyed cuddle bunny, but a big, tough-skinned, thick-kneed jackrabbit. His ears were as long as his body was tall, and his feet were like oversized tennis shoes plopping patterns in the dust of west Texas. Oscar loved to leap over sagebrush and tickle low clouds with his ears and cover the distance across highways with one bounce.

One day Oscar got an invitation to dine with the king, and Oscar was so pleased that he tied his ears in a bow knot and hugged the nearest tumbleweed into a dance. "I am invited to dinner with the king," he sang, clutching his invitation to his heart. About that time Puffy Altocroaker, who was a peacock, rustled over to see what all the fuss was about, and Oscar told her he had been invited to dinner with the king.

Puffy asked, in a haughty tone, what Oscar was going to wear to the king's dinner, and Oscar said he hadn't even thought about that. Puffy went into great detail about just how one must look and act to be welcome into the king's presence.

"Watch me," Puffy said. "You have to stretch your neck high, point your toes together, and spread feathers into a fan." She tossed several little stones for Oscar to place within his toes to make him walk properly for the king. She selected two feathers she had dropped, and with her curved beak helped Oscar pierce through his tough skin to connect the bright feathers to his arms. Oscar was in a lot of pain, but Puffy told him he was now ready to meet the king and to keep practicing with the stones in his toes so he could walk properly.

It took Oscar a long time to get to the king's party, and he was afraid he was going to be late for the dinner, but he was met by a duck in a swaddle-tailed jacket who told him he was just in time. The king came to greet Oscar, and Oscar tried to bow, but he couldn't do that properly without losing his balance because of the stones in his toes and the feathers stuck in his arms. The worst part was that the king didn't recognize him at first, and Oscar had to whisper to the duck in the swaddle-tailed jacket that he was Oscar Overstep, invited to dinner with the king. Then the king came to Oscar and looked real close to see who he was, and he welcomed him with a royal hug, but Oscar couldn't hug back because of the feathers and the stones. The king said, "Oscar, I'm so glad you're here. I want to watch you leap over sagebrush and tickle low clouds with your ears and I would enjoy seeing you cover the distance across the highway with one bounce."

Oscar hung his head and whispered to the king, "I can never do that with the stones between my toes and these feathers in my arms. I wore them to be acceptable at your party and proper in your presence, but now I can hardly stand, and even if I had the strength to leap a little, I'd surely lose these feathers doing it."

The king, who loved Oscar, called the duck in the swaddle-tailed jacket to help get rid of the feathers, and the king himself knelt to slip the stones from Oscar's toes. And then the king said softly to Oscar, "Oh, dear Oscar, you didn't read the invitation. It said very clearly, Come as you are."

The moral of the story is all about grace and invitations and not paying too much attention to peacocks.

CHAPTER 10

Survival in the Storm

*M*y husband and I lived for many years in an apartment building. One evening, leaving from its front door, we saw a small crowd of frantic people surrounding a car parked at the steps. In the backseat of the car was a young baby. The baby's mother had run hurriedly into the building to leave a package for a resident and had inadvertently locked the car. She was now frantically calling locksmiths and finding none. Around the car were a dozen people, all focused on the baby. Two of the worried adults had gone up to their apartment to claim two musical toys now being loudly played against the locked window of the backseat. Another adult had a flashing wand waving from the other window at the little child who, unused to such attention, was crying loudly.

One of the adults said, "We have to quiet the baby, his crying is taking up the oxygen inside the car." It was a hot midsummer evening with the sun still winning its battle with the shade. Someone brought a hammer, but was cautioned against its use for fear the baby would be cut by the falling glass, and so the games played against the windows continued. Attempts to involve the child in a quick game of patty-cake were met with more crying. The flashing wand beat against the window. The musical toys were joined by other instruments, and against the steady rhythm of the mother's crying, a small orchestra was loudly in force.

I noticed my husband standing at a distance surveying the scene, as was his usual habit when confronted with a crisis. Then he spoke to one of the men just outside the circle around the car. The two men conferred for a few seconds and then moved to the back of the car and with gentle but persistent pressure, removed the back window, and immediately the mother reached in and got her baby out. Later the police, a fire engine, and three locksmiths appeared; but the crisis was over. The baby was out. The police and fire departments were there as soon as they heard they were needed, but the crisis was resolved by my husband, who was not focused on entertaining the child but on getting the child out.

I serve in the business of entertainment. I can unroll a list of people whose lives have been bettered by the application of healthy entertainment administered to various ailments suffered in our time—audience members comforted by the unique fellowship of attending theater, specific problems addressed by statements enacted on the stage, young people sharing a strategy for health as offered in the company's touring programming, wonderful experiencing of the realistic healing of laughter. I believe in theater, but in the instance of the baby locked in the car, the need was not to entertain the locked-in but to get the locked-in out.

Much can be done in the silence of God to get the locked-in out and the locked-out in. Despair and defeat and diminishing of self need to be locked out. But the call to service, the reaching out to the needs of others, the sharing of God with others need never be locked out. I am a Christian, and I dearly love the fellowship of faith. I honor and respect the church, the body of Christ and all its Christ-centered units of individual churches. However, I have a concern that believers secured by the enclosing of Christ are growing less aware of the world outside our shelter. Correctly canceling the world's authority over us, we also may incorrectly cancel our ministry to the world.

Faith is not passive.

Peace is not apathy.

Love is not withdrawal.

One of the mistakes we make when under the cloud of God's silence is to think that since God seems to have nothing to say to us, he has said nothing that validates his pauses. His pauses can strengthen us in the noise of the world's talk to us. The world is never going to validate your faith intentionally, but it may do it unintentionally. In fact, God himself sometimes uses the unbelieving world to affirm and often define the believer's faith.

We often say, "God will use you if you will give your life to him." The fact is that God will use you whether or not you give your life to him. He is not off in some crowded corner of his heavens, biting his holy fingernails for fear your unbelief will interfere with his divine plans. God uses whom he chooses. He used twisted, tainted, tyrannical Pharaoh just as clearly as he used Moses. However, he used Pharaoh like dead wood, a puppet. He used Moses as a contributing human individual. In the same way God often chooses to use the unbeliever unto the believer's benefit.

I have known times when Satan overplayed his hand, and I saw clearly the evil purposes of his devices. We Christians often are identified by the opposition, a result the opposition never intended. But what the devil thought was a choice weapon turned out to be a boomerang; and boom, it rang against him and for us. However, with all the assurances of God's over-turning, the world will never intentionally affirm the believer's faith. And that can make situational faith difficult.

When God is silent, the opposition to him is on a talking jag. I can assure you, in the silence of God, every doubt you ever had will strut across the stage of your mind. Aha! Some lingering suspicion of theology's rhetoric will be magnified. Everything you have not liked about your fellow believers will be accented. And what was a whisper of self-doubt will become a four-alarm siren: you aren't smart enough, haven't read enough, haven't been to enough seminars, don't know enough to have a reasonable conviction about Jesus, God, his Word, his church, the Holy Spirit, or the newest Christian catalog from James Avery. And from outside the boiling pot of your mind, in the silence, you will hear, directly or indirectly, major attack questions, such as:

1. Who do you think you are to judge the world's multitudes of unbelievers?
2. I can't believe you believe the Bible. I read it, and it left me cold. What do you say to that?
3. How do you support your belief in the face of suffering?

Every once in a while I think of sharp and even clever retorts because I am invigorated by the debate. I had been a debater against him, so I thought I was well prepared to be a debater for him. Then God quietly informed me I was more eager to win the argument than to win the arguer. There were other limitations, like that specific verse in Ephesians (4:15), which means that if I cannot love that person who dares to question my faith, chances are this would be a good time for me to say nothing.

The good news is, there are more grand books of godly answers to such questions than there are ungodly questions. Haddon Robinson, Josh McDowell, Charles Swindoll, Earl Palmer, Philip Yancey, Cynthia Heald, and Jill Briscoe are just a few in the cloud of witnesses writing today who have solid answers for those questions.

From me, here are a few:

Question: Who do you think you are to judge the world's multitudes of unbelievers?

Answer: I don't. In fact, I just checked over my list of assignments from God, and judging isn't on the list at all. Not of people and their right to heaven or proclivity for hell. I can judge essay papers, I can

judge whether the stylish new shoe is worth the pain
it causes my feet. I make such choices every day, and
my judgment selections are generally important to me.
But I do not have the assignment of judging others as
to their stand before God. Nor do I think the world's
multitude of unbelievers have the option for judging
me on the basis of my faith.

Question: I can't believe you believe the Bible.
I read it, and it left me cold. What do you say to that?

Answer: As to your reaction to the Bible, I'm not
particularly thrown by that. I also rejected it, and that
rejection left me cold. It was the Bible that got me out
of the cold and into the warmth of his love.

Question: How do you support your belief in the
face of suffering?

Answer: In the face of suffering, I offer compassionate understanding and the promise of fellowship
with the living God who chose to enter the domain of
our suffering to get us out from under its authority.
I also believe that God does not disengage himself
from our sorrows and rule dispassionately from a
distance. I offer him to the sufferer because he, a man
of sorrows, acquainted with grief, is quick to help in
time of need.

Sometimes silence does a good thing. It gets us in touch
with our questions, and those questions may be the nearest
point of contact with the unbeliever.

I find it sad when we in the Christian community become so delighted with our answers that we close the shutters and lock ourselves in and away from the dialogue. I think we need to be in the dialogue with compassion and respect and with our homework done. There is no need to put ourselves at the mercy of the world's arguing dialogue. That is a waste of time as well as energy and places us in a dangerous, vulnerable position. I seriously doubt that God sends us out into the world to win arguments, but he does send us out to win the lost.

I had to get this old before I learned what would have helped me get this old more gracefully. Not all questions have answers, not all hurts heal, and not all broken parts mend. If you are demanding a life that has only answerable questions, healed hurts, and mended broken parts, you will miss the adventure of life as it is and stumble badly over your first unanswerable question.

Part of the worthiness of God is that he himself holds us when our grasp falters within the mystery of questions and hurts and broken parts. Past my questions, I found him. Within the hurt, I found him. And without him none of my broken parts would ever be mended. That is what I can share of my faith. I came into the fellowship of the Lord Jesus with questions. I still have questions but no doubts. The self-determined doubter probably will not be calmed by answers because his determination to doubt will always find more questions. It's like anger. A loose translation of a proverb says, "If you rescue an angry man from the water, you will have an angry man on the shore!" The difference between an angry man and a man who is angry is enormous! Committed to doubt we hear no answers.

But for the questions of a storm-tossed generation, Jesus is the shore.

The silence of God may give you a common question to establish communication to an uncommon faith.

Shortly after the film *The Hiding Place* was distributed, I found myself frequently asked questions Corrie ten Boom would know and I didn't. Not knowing has never kept me from answering, so I swung my wavering bat at every one of them. I regret the error and the confusion I must have caused.

God will not hold you accountable for information he has not given you. He knows the speed of the bike he gave us and will not command us to pedal faster than our bike can run.

I am not proficient in the matter of computers. Frustrated by the problems in my home computer, I transferred to one at the office and found it made the same mistakes the one in my home did! One night when I was groaning over the mistakes from my computer, Lorraine, my husband, declared that the next day we were going to get me a new one. That is the always complimentary attitude of my husband concerning my proficiency. But I explained to him that was like buying a new television set because you don't like the program on the old one.

Once we were dining in a fine restaurant, and I ordered a baked potato. It came with a small package of seasoned sour cream, placed on a little silver tray. I fumbled with the package trying to open it and finally squashed it in its middle. Seasoned sour cream squirted like a fire hose covering a block of fire. I was covered with it. The next table was covered with it. The thick, plush carpet was covered with it, and Lorraine had a small stripe of it on his face. He immediately moved to fix my splattered needs and called the head waiter. That gentleman came quickly, and Lorraine gave him an authoritative look and pronounced, "You gave my wife a defective sour cream packet." With many defective packages and several inoperative computers, I have begun to suspect which one of us is in error.

A frequent problem with my computer is the matter of highlighting special paragraphs. Yesterday I highlighted two sentences. Unable to unhighlight the rest of my work, my completed manuscript was all highlight and lost the emphasis I needed. God never makes that mistake. He prints out, for our daily assignments, just the amount of information highlighted for our needs. He never gives us assignments beyond our capacity. But he expects us to put into practice what he has taught.

I see us as little birdlings tucked into the nest. It's comfy. And then suddenly God hands us a full suit of armor. We thank him for thinking of us but, chirping happily in the warmth of the nest, explain to him we don't need those awkward things like helmets and swords, and besides they just don't fit in the nest. And then what God says almost shocks us into the maturity we hadn't planned on accomplishing. He says gently at first that he hadn't planned for us to stay in the nest, and where we're going we will need every stitch of the armor and shield and power-heavy sword.

He who has already said and done enough to take us through the silence and into the dialogue of life sends us out into the world not merely to make a statement for God but to be a statement from God. A vigorous statement, energized and energetic, focusing on the selective exercise of gifts and opportunities. God is not at work equipping a museum with posture-static saints, nor is he hiding us in the depth of the ground like some long-forgotten pirate treasure. We are to be not merely receivers of his gifts but active conduits of their treasure. The God who might for a time be silent is still to be at all times obeyed. And for the purpose of our obedience, we can be assured he not only has answers; he *is* the answer.

I need to clarify the point that there are times and instances when the Christian loses continuity with the world and its citizens. There are times and instances when breaking the ties that bind to the unbelieving community is tantamount to obedience. The Christian needs the church, its resources, its comfort, its protection, and its unique encouragement. It is dangerous for the believer to abandon or to deprioritize Christian fellowship. Sometimes the most stalwart and mature believer can lose his moorings when his little ship drifts outside the harbor of the church and its discipline.

There are other instances when the believer's hand, reaching out through the definitive markings of his belief, may be the relief agency for that part of our world and a relieving of tension for the world of which we are a part. And it may be that God Almighty is waiting silently for that outreaching hand.

The comfort of Christian fellowship can become insular for many reasons. Some of the reasons are not only valid; they are essential. But some of the reasons do not match God's intention.

> The particular calling of a particular believer
> may, by its signature, isolate him from the ebbing and
> flowing of the world.

The focus of this same calling may, by its demands, preclude activity with the world outside its primary focus.

The vigorous scheduling of the active Christian life can eliminate times of work or fellowship outside its dimensions.

The Christian can become so focused on the dictum of his faith that he loses the facility of dialogue with those who don't share it.

I find the first two valid and the last two questionable as they can result in a loss of perception as to people. We begin to catalog and abruptly reject this broad spectrum of humanity who, by the choice of God, occupy this planet with us at this particular time. Regardless of the faith of our decision, we live out that faith amid ordinary humanity, not carrying identifying posters as to their faith but all branded as people.

I am the artistic director of a Christian theater company. That vigorous company occupies much of my time and interest. Its needs are always highly prioritized in my consideration. However, if I begin to see people only as potential donors, possible auxiliary, or future members, I have degraded the value of people as people, isolated myself, and actually failed to represent the organization for which I rendered myself exclusive.

People are people. Some are good; some are bad. Some are villains, and some are heroes. Some are to be cultivated in friendship, and some are to run from in even slight association. But we live in a world populated by people, and when the eager

Christian sees all people as nothing but a mission field, I think he loses his perspective of humanity.

I spoke some time ago at a program in which one of the speakers, an excellent speaker and Christian leader, asked how many of the Christians there had brought unbelievers. Several raised their hands and were applauded. I was impressed by the outreach of those Christians. They had stepped out from their Christian comfort zone to bring in their friends. The applause was valid. We need to be about the business of such action. But I squirmed for the visitors who may have just learned they were trophies and not friends.

There are people of a faith not mine who come to my door to enlist me in the fellowship they believe is the only one of value. They come smiling and friendly with attractive and well-organized material. I admire their commitment to their belief although I find the elements of that belief riddled with critical error. I admire their focused ministry, but I know they are not at my door for my benefit but for theirs. By winning me, they win not only brownie points for this life but a sure seat in the grandstand of heaven.

There are valid reasons for the believer to isolate himself from the general category of people, and I have nothing but the deepest respect for those who follow those reasons. But I feel that isolating calling is occasionally shared by those who have not been so called.

Dale Chapman, a friend and fellow coworker in Christian assignments, said of Christ that one of the most amazing of his attributes was that he was comfortable in the presence of sinners. I see Jesus overturning the tables of the money changers.

I read the term applied to his dissenters as an evil and adulterous generation. I ache over the results of his proclamation of himself as Messiah, and yet I also stand in the bushes outside Simon's house and hear the Pharisees' damning criticism of Jesus because he was having a good time at a party that included sinners.

It is a sensitive issue to be in the world and not of it. When my faith excludes me from fellowship with those who do not share it, and often it does, may it be their exclusion and not my signed exclusivity.

When I chartered my theater course to be Christian, many of my theater friends thought I had dropped off the ends of the earth and was so removed from theater there was no hope of ongoing communication. That hurt me deeply. But some of my theater friends left the gate open, and we fellowshipped in theater, which is actually what we do. Some of those came with me into faith; some did not. I have friends who are believers and friends who are not. I pray for both categories but often emphasize the latter with great intensity.

One such unbelieving friend I often called my favorite pagan. She knew I was a Christian, and I knew she was not. We worked in theater together, roomed together at one time in New York, and started our two theaters at much the same time. One day I flew to the city where she was, and we shared an hour's visit before I returned home. I told her I wanted to be sure that within the activities of our friendship I had clearly offered her the gospel. And seated eye-to-eye with her, I went through the specifics of Christ's gospel as though speaking to one who had never heard it before. My friend held my hand after my talk and said, "Yes, Jeannette, I have heard it. You have presented it, and I have heard it. I do not believe it, but you can rest assured I have heard it."

Our friendship continued, and I don't think I ever detailed the gospel again. I spoke at her funeral because she had asked me to do that. To that large group assembled, I spoke of my friend as a believer because one night, years after our eye-to-eye talk, she called me. It was long distance and late at night. She was concerned by the overpowering trend of evil in the world and felt helpless as her native goodness recognized such negative power. I told her the only power I knew against evil was God, and over the phone my friend accepted Jesus as her Savior. It was specific, it was clear, and her letters to me afterward spoke of it as life changing. The friendship maintained is now eternal fellowship. Had I lost her friendship when I defined the gospel, I would have lost eternal fellowship.

I have in my home several battery-powered night-lights plugged into my hall, my bedroom, and two near the front door. Most of them have attractive designs—a teacup, a happy face, an angel, and a small clock. In the light I am only casually aware of them, but in a recent storm one crackling lightning flash turned off all my electricity. I was in darkness except for my glowing night-lights and the small flashlight I keep by my bed. In the light we are to check our batteries, but in the dark we are to shine. The power is in the light. If we are not drawing power from the light, there is no hope for us in the darkness. And in the blackness and its encompassing silence in the storm, I heard a clicking noise. It was from the night-light that includes a clock. And then I heard dimly, as though from far away, music. It was from that same-night light. It has a clock *and* a radio.

What are we to do in this shadowed world with its storms and scariness and sometimes silence? It's really simple. Keep careful watch over our batteries, and be ready in the dark to provide light and time and music.

🎔 *Dear Lord,*
There's this little verse in Philippians. It seems to indicate that you
want me to be a light. How can that be? I'm afraid of the dark. And
I volunteered to shine where the light is, not where it's not! And then, Lord,
there's a verse that is so difficult. What do you mean about not grumbling
or arguing? I do these things so well and shine in the dark so poorly that it
would seem to me your directions are inappropriate. However, there is that
other verse, the one that encourages me every time I read it. In that verse
you remind me that you are at work in me that I might not only do your
bidding but want to do your bidding. It's working, God. I want to shine
where you place me and know what time it is in the dark. And in the
silence I want to hear your music.
Amen.
Philippians 2:12–15

Memo

His name was William, and he was every minute of five years old. He was excited about going to his friend's birthday party. Oscar, his friend, was to be five years old. William's first selection while shopping was the large brown bear with rotating head and sparkling eyes stationed at the front door, but his mother explained to him that the bear was part of the store's insignia and not suitable for giving.

The gift chosen was a fire truck with big red wheels that whistled as they rolled. William assisted his mother in wrapping the gift and even signed the card himself with big, wobbly letters. William held the gift carefully as they drove to the birthday party and eagerly rang the doorbell and bounded into the house as Oscar and his mother greeted him. And then it happened! William's mother cued him to give the gift to Oscar, and William refused.

To William, choosing the gift, wrapping the gift, and signing the gift card did not mean relinquishing the gift. The entry hall was a noisy place. William's mother gave the wrapped fire truck to Oscar's mother, and William refused the happy hat and did not participate in the gaiety of the party until halfway through the chocolate cake and ice cream. In fact, his departure from the party was somewhat sullen.

Absurd! Childish! Shame on William! Of course everyone knows that gifts are to be given! Participating in the selection, the wrappings, and the signing are merely tokens of grace because the gifts supplied by God are in transit, to be given freely with joy and no regrets. Of course, everyone knows that! Or do we?

CHAPTER 11

Sometimes When God Says Nothing, It May Mean Nothing

When I was a little girl, I made up this phrase from the jargon of adults, "Everything is happening to once." It was heard as cute from my six-year-old lips and became a family classic comment. Now my older lips recite it, and it is not cute. Indeed, I live in a season when everything is happening to once, and I have a disturbing feeling that I may be the "once" to whom everything is happening. Priorities get juggled, needs get recataloged, schedules melt in the heat of realities, and I live my life habitually interruptible. Those whose lives fit comfortably into their scheduled priorities have no sympathy for me because they have no experiential understanding. I took the courses, I read the chapters, I outlined the programs; but I still live under the authority of crises, and that is not good.

Some few times the jumble of assignments creates such a bedlam that the silence of God is vaguely comforting. At least he has nothing to say, nothing to request, and no suggestion that will in its time produce more assignments. However, I need his voice over the tumult of lesser beings, and I must choose to lower their volume to lift his.

What to do when everything is happening to once, and only God is silent? I may not have a certain answer, but I am sympathetic with the question, and I share a few principles for more than marginal survival.

Prioritizing Ownership

Take the time to disentangle yourself from that which you do not own. Compassion is an assignment of grace. Without it life dies in many ways and at different speeds. It is the crème de la crème of love and must be preserved at any cost, but I have found that too many needs crying for attention can dry up the flow of my compassion and in time turn on the faucets of bitterness.

Prioritize ownership. Are there services you require of yourself that are not really owned by you? Even Mother Teresa couldn't reach them all. There may be some assignment picked up as priority that can be demoted. I am an inveterate fixer, not a successful one but a habitual one. I have faced a disturbing fact. I am not so eager to fix the problem as I am eager to become the one who fixed it. Who appointed me sovereign stabilizer of the world? Nobody. Least of all God.

I now consider the fact that some of the pressures clinging like barnacles to the hub of my life are not only not mine or my assignment; but by embracing them with what I think is compassion, I am deterring their process to the resources that may indeed fix them. Clinging stubbornly to a job not mine, I am never a hero but often a stumbling block.

One Easter performance in our theater was rudely interrupted by a power failure in the midst of the program. The stage lights dimmed and darkened. I, watching from the back of the house, immediately rushed to the stairs leading to the light booth. Scrambling in the dark, I pulled myself into the small area where Sissy, our production manager, was at work.

"What are you doing here?" she asked.

"The lights are going out!" I answered.

"I know that," she said, "but what are you doing here?"

The truth is as the truth was: I know nothing about stage lighting, and Sissy knows all there is to know about it. I was but an unnecessary addition to the crisis. And also unnecessary to its resolution, which was going on very well without me and needed the space my noncontributing presence was occupying.

When God is silent in the happenings "to once," check to see if you need be where you are and if the needs need you. What are you doing here?

I hate to admit it, but occasionally when everything is happening at once, I falsely assume everything is suddenly my business. I find myself dramatically, actively, and most often loudly involved in what is not my call from God or from the human-type person I rush to answer. In such times God is silent only as a hint for me to respond similarly. In order to help the situation, one of us should stop talking, and chances are that one of us is me.

Try prioritizing ownership. Are all those problems really yours? If that doesn't work, try the clutter cure.

The Clutter Cure

People who make good money telling other people how to rid their lives, garages, closets, and offices of clutter generally specialize in the one-at-a-time theory. "Rid your house of five things a day, and at the end of the year your house will be clutter free." That's what it says on the poster as a young aproned woman leans gently upon a broom, smiling at the well-organized home around her. For me it did not work. When I took five things out, I immediately brought six things in. However, life is not a swap meet. Try the clutter cure.

Select three (not five—we don't want to get well all of a sudden), three buzzing consequential worries that keep you awake at night. Give each of them an uninterrupted hour of your time. Let the others wait. In that hour do, delegate or dismiss what can be done, delegated, or dismissed. At the end of the day, you may find those delayed by the exercise have either given up or are still waiting. You will also find that at least one of the things you focused on is in better condition, and all you now have to contend with is the guilt for spending three hours missing all that did not have your focus. Now address the guilt face-to-face with God. If it is truly a sin, confess it. If it is an error, correct it. And if face-to-face with God it doesn't really matter, forget it and go on to the next set of three.

In the discovery that neither the clutter cure nor the prioritizing work for you, try a bold and courageous step. Risk asking someone whose opinion you respect if you give evidence of being productive.

Productivity wears many different hats and not always a readable name tag. God does not identify one's productivity by someone else's productivity. His silence is not necessarily his holy critique of our performance. That critique may be self-inflicted, and the silence of God is simply because he finds no agreement with the critique. Ask that trusted friend if there is reason to believe you are productive in the midst of the happenings that confound you. If the answer is no, ask someone else.

Try at least two other people before accepting the fact that your worst fears are valid and then action must be taken to change you or the circumstances. However, if the answer is yes, there is a good possibility that this swarming of happenings is just the system that renders you most productive. It may be that you do your best under pressure; and it is God, who knows you best, who is doing the pressing. The good news is that if this yes is true and you address it properly, the anxiety, which is not pleasing to God, can be dismissed. The paralysis of anxiety is gone, and in its place you can celebrate productivity with peace, excitement with faith, and God's sovereignty with his gift of employment. And when you can't sleep, instead of counting the wrinkles of worry, simply praise his holy name.

The prophet Jeremiah is special to me. Bless his weeping heart! He flunked Positive Thinking 103 and went on to do graduate work in Truth Telling. Overwhelmed by his assignment, he said, "Enough is enough."

> He decided to quit but couldn't.
> He prayed for his people and shouldn't.
> He stood for truth when others wouldn't.

And when all was said and done, he mapped out hope in the most glorious way.

The situation of his service could not have been worse. The people of God, precious in his sight, were dancing around pagan altars, worshipping trees and molten gods they had made. Forsaking the water of life, they were drinking from man-made sewers and complaining of thirst. And preaching Jeremiah was voted the most hated man of the year. Everything bad was happening "to once" for Jeremiah. And yet, and strangely enough because of it, Jeremiah poured out jewels of hope, glittering like freshly cut diamonds in the mire of desolate circumstances.

To say Jeremiah was overwhelmed is an understatement. He began his ministry with an apology, served his ministry grieving, suffered being stuffed into a pit, and yet was so productive that you and I today can ignite our flickering fires from sparklers of Jeremiah's wisdom. Sometimes you have to lose what you think is the best of you to learn the true value of the rest of you. Through Jeremiah, God said, "I know the plans I have for you, and they are good."

You may not be able to praise God wholeheartedly for everything happening "to once," but you can praise God in the everything. Yes, you can! I know it, I have done it.

Try this prayer:

✿ *Dear God,*

If this, which to me seems overwhelming, is where you have placed me for your good purposes, then I accept this as my place. You know what is best for me, and what pleases you pleases me. All I ask is that in this and through this and in spite of this, I hear you. In contact with you, even the "once" of many happenings is but a workshop in the temple, with the light shining through the stained-glass windows. Little dapplings of that light touch my hands like childhood's freckles. I give to you my handiwork. It is far from perfect, gnarled with mistakes and patterned with confusion. But in your light, even it may become productive.

Amen.

CHAPTER 12

Jacob Wasn't the Only One with a Lame Excuse

It was a clumsy but casual incident. With my arms full of files relating to a radio program, I slid into a chair awkwardly and twisted my ankle. It hurt, but I judged it a minor accident. An ice pack was immediately applied, and I resumed the day's activity as planned. I was to leave at six the next morning for a speaking engagement in Virginia. That afternoon I participated in a children's program and hurried home to pack for the next morning's early departure. The pain increased. I could no longer stand on the aching foot and knew I needed help. Proverbs tells us a brother is born for adversity. I add that friends often stick closer than 911. Two friends took me to the emergency room of a nearby hospital.

The doctor defined the tennis-ball-size swollen flesh at my ankle joint as a sprained ankle and presented me with crutches, medication, and a solemn demand to stay off the offended foot for the next twenty-four hours. My Virginia trip was cancelled, and I went home to spend twenty-four idle hours eyeing the crutches and fearful that, while processing them, worse things than a sprained ankle might befall me.

Physical inactivity usually encourages bursts of mental activity, and I found the time for a lengthy session of self-accusation. While my ankle healed, my spirit sickened. I had failed. It is part of my nature to see to it that as far as my commitments go, the show must go on. I have played shows with a broken rib, walking pneumonia, family in crisis, a collapsing set, and five hundred invitations to my wedding still to be mailed. I have taken great pride in the fact that in spite of the circumstances I can be trusted to show up. And now in one short evening, I had proven myself to be unreliable.

Unable to cope with pain, I had failed a commitment. When I looked at that failing, I noted several other failures I had been too busy to consider, but now they paraded like marching drummers cued for a grand entrance. That negative orchestration hurt more than my ankle. Small failings, major failings. Known failings, never revealed failings. In the crisis of inactivity, all my failings demanded my full attention. Significant beginnings that had fallen far short of their intentions. Choices I had made in moments of decision that resulted in hours and days of grievous results. I began to think painfully of the myth that was me. There was a space between my true identity and the person I was thought to be. Those who liked me did not really know who I was, and the people who did not like me did not know what I was not. The conclusion was worse than failure; it was a solemn verdict of fraudulence. While I negated myself, there was no one to speak otherwise. I was a fraud, a failure, and a fool.

The fear of fraudulence is a common fear. It is as old as the history of man. It was first served with the applesauce in the garden of Eden. It may be the result of mishandled funds, the precariousness of worldly success, sudden popularity that depends on some event that happened to grant prestige, or the long-protected myth that we had become godlike, when all the time we knew differently. It takes little to light its smoking torch—a friend's casual remark, an awkward loneliness, failure to measure up. And suddenly we peer into the magnified image of our fraudulence—uncovered, discovered, and turned over.

As a relatively public figure, I often am told confidentially of personal needs. Because I come and go without the aftermath of lingering relationship, strangers will share with me what they would never confide to their friends. And without a doubt, that which I most often hear is an aching, debilitating, self-deduced fraudulence. Famous actresses, successful executives, the recently promoted or temporarily demoted express the fear of fraudulence revealed. I share my feelings not because of their unique significance but because of their mundane commonality.

How dare I stand before the public as a Christian speaker when I knew in my heart I was a fraud. Fraudulent not just because I had failed to show up in Virginia, but because of the times I had shown up in public with false credentials. I dare to tell others of the need for mentally storing up Bible knowledge but keep three concordances handy or I would never find my favorite Scriptures. I teach the values of preparation, processing, and patience, and I falter in the practice of each of them.

I recently exited a plane and found a friend had also been on that flight and during it had led three people to the Lord while I was working on a crossword puzzle. A crossword puzzle instead of saving the multitudes.

I have a small plaque honoring me as a communicator, and after an hour's staff meeting under my communication I learned no one had understood what in the world I was talking about.

A dear friend facing surgery gave me the time and place of the event that she might be assured of my prayers during the operation. I promised and forgot the schedule and prayed at the wrong time for the wrong hospital, and my friend said she felt my prayer watch throughout the hours of the crisis. I smiled and said I was glad to be a part of her recovery. I have failed my friends, failed my job, and failed my God.

I called out in prayer, "Oh God, here I am—a fraud, a failure, and a fool." And God was silent. Through my tears I listened, and he said nothing.

The next morning I hobbled to church. It was an unusually effective sermon. I felt the comfort of the music and the fellowship but knew such comfort was undeserved. The Scripture was vivid but singularly inappropriate to my dilemma. Everybody else was where he was supposed to be. I was supposed to be in Virginia participating in a carefully planned program, and I was not. With just a little effort and some quick lessons in crutchery, I could have done my job. Seven hundred people gathering at a church in Virginia had been disappointed because I succumbed to the hindrance of pain. Oh God, I failed to keep a commitment. I am a fraud, a failure, and a fool.

And God was silent.

Because I was to have been in Virginia, someone other than me was teaching my Bible class. I went to the class and was grateful for the grace of welcome. In the prayer I reminded God that I was a fraud and a failure, but no one knew it but him and me; and since he was silent, I could get by for at least a Sunday.

Mike Massey, the director of the class, taught an excellent lesson. I relished it and heard again about the fishermen who were cleaning their nets after a night of futile fishing. They had caught nothing. Packing up what was not productive is a depressing thing to do. People were watching, and so was Jesus. He told them it wasn't time to quit but time to leave the shallow water and go out into the deep. That must have been hard on Peter. Fishermen don't like being tutored by carpenters, but they obeyed and caught so many fish that their nets almost broke.

And Jesus never said a word about their failure. In fact, he did not speak to them as though they were failures, fraudulent, and foolish. He spoke to them as though they were fishermen.

Mike's lesson was wonderful. He taught many other things, including a principle I had never heard before. He encouraged us not to pray for the revealing of God's plan for our lives but the revealing of the plan of God that we might fit our plan for our lives into it.

That's not so easy to accept. Some of our best plans don't fit in his. The apostle Paul tells us that some of his best plans did not fit in the holy purposes of God. In Paul's letter to the Philippians, he says that not only did he have to discard some of his most credible plans, but he considered the stuff that didn't fit in worthless. That is an enormous statement and a chilling wake-up call to the stumbling, fumbling, humbling Christ follower. What doesn't fit in God's suitcase doesn't make the trip of God's itinerary. Don't grieve over what God leaves out, or you'll leave out the value of what God puts in.

Our plans are needful to the disciplined adventure of living, but they don't always fit into the plan of God. And there I was, condemned by the failure of my plan, the weakness of my strength, and the foolishness of my errors. And there God was, adjusting my plan to his, balancing my weakness with his strength, and leading me through my foolishness to his wisdom.

And God was no longer silent. In fact, he had never been silent. I had come to him with the wrong name tag. He did not have me listed in his holy file under *fraudulent* or *failure* or *foolish*. He had me listed only under *forgiven*.

God can find me wherever I am. The cover-up of my hidings does not faze him. He can find me lurking in the filth of the pigsty, languishing behind feather fans in a palace, digging a bunker in a sandpit. None of those addresses is outside his map search. His finding me and identifying me is not the trouble; the trouble is my identifying me wherever I am as his.

I am a child of the living God. I make a lot of mistakes, behave foolishly, and at times miss the mark of accuracy, but those errors don't define me. I may have the effects of those errors in my life but not their condemnation. My name tag as a child of the living God grants me access to confession and forgiveness without losing my name tag—and a place in the boat with the rest of his fishers.

I may not know a bait box from a boom box. All I know of casting may be assigning actors their parts in a play. I may be cleaning up a net that has not been sullied by a single fish, but I am still a fisher who needs to get out of the shallow waters of self-condemnation and into the open waters of the deep.

Go all the way back to Adam hiding in the bushes of his sin and hear God speaking, "Where are you?" What are you doing making camp in the shadows of your mistakes? The Bible tells us God knows we are frail; that is not the problem. The fact that we are frail is not news to God. The ultimate problem is not discovering that we are frail; the ultimate problem is forgetting that he is not.

All believers must never forget that we are sinners. Without that reminder we lose the glory of grace. I do not dismiss the need for accountability. It is a rough and painful necessity. Living outside his will for our lives is doom driven. But God will go to any lengths to get his child back into a working relationship with him—not just because the fishing is good but because the fellowship is even better.

Does God seem silent when you come to him in the hopeless equation of your mistakes? When we come to him cloaked with self-praise and puffed out of shape with self-righteousness, we will always find a silent God. But we also miss the sound of his voice when our faith finds its focus on our errors rather than on his power.

The silence of God may be in the echoes of self-condemnation. Fraudulence claimed can even be sound-proofing, and the whisper of his mercy is well worth hearing. Hush the listings of condemnations forgiven.

Listen. The God who loves you is now speaking. Don't miss a word.

Memo

My mother was a concert pianist, but her giftedness was not given to her daughter. I often long to bring music from my mother's piano, which stands waiting in the living room; and once in a while, usually early in the morning, I go to that piano and play a few chords or a one-finger-stroking of a favorite melody and sometimes sing along with my uncertain music.

This morning my solo performance had accompaniment; the beagles next door joined in with a hearty beagle-baying, our morning woodpecker started his staccato treatment on our front balcony, and the orchestration was amplified with the humming of a lawn mower across the street and a sound of metal tapping metal that came from the house building on the corner.

I kept up the stressing of chords, adding a glissando up and then down the keyboard, finished with a flourish, and sat back to listen to the other sounders of their music. One by one they ceased their sounds; the beagles no longer bayed, the woodpecker flew away, and the high-toned patter of metal upon metal ceased. Only the humming lawn mower continued. The symphony was over. I had thoroughly enjoyed it and bowed to an imaginary audience. Each of us has his or her music, and God loves to orchestrate us.

> What do you bring to the morning?
> What do you bring to your day?
> A song of hope, a sigh of sorrow?
> A greeting tossed on your way?
> What do you bring to the morning?
> What is there in you that sings?
> Let God be the Great Conductor
> And join in the music he brings.

CHAPTER 13

Freedom in Need

One of the great assurances I have learned is that what might
have been, never was. And in the case of the believer, what
might have come from the tenants of the old life never should
have been in the first place. Unresolved echoes have to be
dismissed, or they drown out the voice of God in the present.
Reconsidering choices in the past forms hard wax in the ears
and has to be treated with critical attention.

Jesus said clearly that freed by him, you and I are free
indeed and consequently free and in deed. However, there is a
tempting trap left at the lid of deliverance by the evil one. He
knows you are out and free, but he doesn't give up. He, the evil
one, wants you wrapped in the trappings, mappings, and toe
tappings of your past condition. He wants you to think like you
used to think, serve him like you used to serve him, and dance

to the rhythm of his music that still resounds from the pit from which you have been delivered.

I am an asthmatic and have been asthmatic since early childhood. Because of the severity of that illness, I missed more school classes than I attended, was not able to participate in sports, and spent many agonized nights struggling for breath. It was awful, but I recovered from it. In fact, my recovery was so evident that the family doctor would call me in to illustrate hope to some worried mother who had just learned her child was asthmatic. I thank the Lord that I can live an active life and seldom think of those years of severe limitation.

However, there are times when in sudden change of temperature, in the height of Houston's allergy season, walking rapidly in the hills of Colorado, in a crowded elevator when someone's perfume assails me, I feel constriction in my chest, a stretching of my neck to breathe, and the slight tingling of a pain that used to affect me critically. In those times panic sends me a hasty telegram. And, strange as it seems, I have known myself to direct me to a full-blown asthma attack when I am not actually having one.

In the first year of my recovery, I had these pseudo attacks often. I am a slow learner, and even now have to tell myself, I am recovered. I exercise caution; I usually have a breathing aid with me. I will not bury my face in a field of new-mown hay, but I am recovered. I have been brought out from under the authority of those symptoms. I do not know what allergies are still in residence. I do not know which of the many treatments I received relieved me. I do not know why other asthmatics my age are still as restricted by the ailment as I was, but I do know that I am recovered and have to tell myself that or the slightest inclination of symptoms will entrap me.

This is not a medical treatise; it is an example of a serious threat to the believer's open communication with God. Reckon with what you have been brought out of, and bring none of its decaying stench with you. In the Bible, when Daniel's stalwart buddies braved the flames of fire rather than amend their faith, they came out of that fire without the smell of smoke. Those boys were smart. They didn't go back into the fire to retrieve a whistle or a whim or a way of wit. They let all that was there burn. God brought them out whole and without even the smell of smoke.

Jesus stood at the grave of Lazarus. He wept at the enormity of death and the price of its ransom. Then to everyone's astonishment he, Jesus, called Lazarus, dead as a four-day doornail, to come out from the grave. And Lazarus did the smartest thing he had ever done; he came out at the command of Jesus. And I think everybody there looked deader than Lazarus. They could not believe what they saw. It was a scary resurrection from known and accepted death.

Jesus' miracles always were and always will be a little upsetting. When Lazarus came out of that tomb, the processing of life was reversed. Death had always been known as final, a tomb not a womb. Lazarus's friends and his sisters were on their way back to the house for the sandwiches and cakes the community would bring, and there before their eyes was Lazarus. And I think Jesus was telling the people, "Don't stand there gaping at my miracle. Do what my miracle has equipped you to do."

Christ, who would use the resurrection of Lazarus to paint a picture of his own resurrection, would also use the obedience of Lazarus to paint a picture of obedience to us. "Do what my miracle has equipped you to do."

And what has the miracle of Lazarus equipped us to do? Jesus said, "Unbind him. Remove the dressings of the grave. Let Lazarus go free." Lazarus was to run, leap, jump, and parade with Jesus in the triumphal entry into Jerusalem. Lazarus was to be a testimony to the power of the Christ. Lazarus was to give answer to his being alive by behaving alive in public. Lazarus could never have done that dressed for the tomb.

The clothes of the grave belong in the grave, not flapping around the ankles of the living. Jesus, who called Lazarus from the tomb, could have taken care of those clinging, scented wrappings with a single word. But he chose to share the activity with the community. He does the same thing today. The community of believers, the church, is God's method for setting the new believer free from the clutter and chatter and clinging of sin. Jesus still says to us who watch with wonder when God himself calls forth a convert, "Unbind him. Let him go free." And when you and I come to the call of Christ, out from under the authority of evil, literally out from the grave, we need be careful not to bring any of the old garments of death.

Why ever would we? Why would anyone go back into the old life and pick up some smelly rotten cloths, a moth-eaten sweater that no longer fits, a collapsed balloon, a rotting walking stick, an out-of-date shawl with tassels so matted they no longer have a pattern of design? Why would anyone go back to the defeated grave to reclaim worthless tokens? Why? Because of habit. To have something habitual and familiar in this newly unfamiliar world. And sadly enough, because they worked so well then. In time habits can be retrained. In growth the new unfamiliar will become familiar. But some of the things we gave up so happily seem appropriate to dealing with matters less than happy now. And those things, those habits, those decorations can cause silences in our communication with the God who brought us from their power.

Don't try to redeem that from which God redeemed you. The technique of the grave does not work for the living. Leave it behind you without a backward look. Disconnect those messages; you are no longer under their authority. Defuse those flashing lights; you are out of the darkness. Forgive them their hurt. Strangely enough God used even those false restrictions to get you to himself. You are recovered. You are rewired. You are newly connected. Identify yourself to yourself and to the defeated tomb.

Soon after each Christmas I receive a small fluttering of Christmas cards returned. Each of them has a stamped imprint of one of several choices: No longer at this address. Forwarding process has expired. Addressee unknown. And all conclude with, Return to sender.

The evil one, who used to have the new believer in his power, sends a lot of mail to the new believer. Some of it is prettily packaged. Some of it has solemn graphics: "This may be your last opportunity to subscribe," or, "This offer is limited, respond immediately," or "Do not throw this away; you may be a winner." Most of it seems personal and suited to our needs (remember the evil one is clever and has had plenty of time to get to know us well), but all of it invites our response. The best response is simple; write on the envelope, "No longer at this address; return to sender."

This is a challenge to those clouded in the silence of God, a challenge I do not always meet.

Life shares with all of us sorrows, pain, and suffering. Those awesome invaders are to be respected and honored with response. Bad things are bad. Suffering is a real occurrence. Pain hurts. Sorrow seeks its own verb. Denial never healed anything. The best it can do is postpone the processing.

Disappointments, despair, and defeat create such a dinning, dimming, condemning noise that we can assume God is silent and we are afloat on a sea of loneliness. God is quick to get through the error to get us out. His Holy Spirit is just as eager to get us back in but this time into service, which can begin in the midst of the silence of God.

Comfort and sorrow seem worlds apart, but they share a common debilitating error. Each of them can render us unresponsive. The comfort of peace can render us apathetic; the comfort of faith can render us idle; and the comfort of love can render us uninvolved. My God is sufficient; my Lord is more than enough. But his sufficiency renders me accountable—not beyond my means, not in comparative holiness (there is no such thing); but if his speaking makes me deaf, his silence can call me to hearing.

In the silence of God, change your venue.

Know for a fact that for you God's silence is temporary, and even in it he is speaking volumes. Assured of that fact, do not dismiss the silence, but let it be for a time, a window. A window through which you can see others suffering the silence of God without his assurance because they lack the information you have. Explore this cage of silence so that you can comfort from your experience the next person engaged in its problem.

Little of the world gets into the Christ-centered believer. We have to claim the interruptions of peace to know what the uninterrupted war outside feels like. I hate to admit it, but I know what it's like not to care one feather about the next person in the line whom I can help. I know what it's like to want only my need met, to resist any interruption of the peace that passes misunderstanding which at the moment I am celebrating. I know what it's like to care more about me being right in the argument than about the rights of the person with whom I am arguing, and I know for a fact that any one of those matters can be a causative for the silence of God. Faith without works is dead—dead silence.

We have been brought out from under the authority of evil, praise the Lord, and then brought most expeditiously into the kingdom of relationship with God through the finished work of the Son of God. For us all things have been made new. A new goal! A new hope! A new modus operandi! And a new language! Believers speak a new language and should never submit themselves again to the authority of the old. But let me tell you something. If a poor lost traveler makes his way to the community of faith from the strategy, stench, and stupor of the pigpen, call the prodigal son. He understands pig Latin. And he, within the security of being in fellowship, can speak out clearly and get the lost in securely.

Recently, and just when I needed it most, I found a brand new Scripture. It must have been there before; a marking of it was in the margin in my handwriting. But my forgettery is often abler than my memory, and the Scripture seemed new. It's a little verse in Jeremiah (15:19), "And if you speak noble [words], rather than worthless ones, you will be My spokesman."

What God has called worthless is worthless. We cannot redeem what he has condemned. If we look back to treasure what he calls waste, if we snatch at the old equipment when he has given us new, if we cling to the outdated attitude instead of stretching to the one freshly given, we have chosen the fashion of the grave and gone against the one who wants us unbound and free. And in refusing the conversation with God's standards, we find him silent in communication with ours. It would be cause for great despair but for God—God calling us through the silence to remind us who we are because he is who he is, and who he is has set us free to be who we are in the celebration of him.

A mysterious word finds its placement in the pages of the Bible only twice, and then with little explanation. The word is *Nehushtan*, which refers to a piece of brass.

Once upon a time in the reality of history, Moses was leading one huge collection of people from Egypt unto Canaan. Although Moses was glad to be out of Egypt and on the way to the promised land, he was not having a good time as leader. The people whom he was leading spent most of their time arguing. Overlooking the fact that Moses had led them out of a dreadful captivity, which would most certainly have been the death of them had they stayed, they turned on Moses at every bend in the road. They got so far as the Red Sea and saw the water in front of them and Pharaoh behind them, and rather than settling down for an evening of choruses around the campfire, they flung all sorts of insults at Moses and told him he should never have forced them out of Egypt.

Then when God parted the waters and the whole bunch of them wagon-loaded and waltz-footed on dry land over to the other side, they started singing and praising God until dinnertime when they found out there wasn't any dinner. Then they sang one more chorus of "We Should Never Have Left Egypt" while Moses did his best to get them back to the table for the best baked manna any of them had ever had. In fact, they had never had manna before—baked, fried, or sautéed with ginger and raisin sauce. God was blessing them with newness at every turn, but it was easier for God to get his people out of captivity than it was to get captivity out of his people.

It's the same with us today. We want to be delivered—oh, yes—but we tend to carry stuff with us that would be better left behind. Stuff like bitterness and willfulness and mean-spirited thinking and worshipping the gods we have made rather than the one God who made us.

Once, while Israel was dragging the wheels of the carriages through all sorts of wanderings and not sending Moses so much as a thank-you note for his good services and not having much good to say about God either, they got impatient because the journey was taking a good deal longer than they had bargained for. And God was eager to get them on to the next campground, so he raised up a bunch of fiery serpents who bit a bunch of the people, and those people died. That got the general attention back on recognizing God, and he had Moses make a fiery serpent out of bronze that worked against snakebite whenever the person bitten looked at that serpent thing raised high on a standard—high like a cross on a hillside. It was a picture, a pattern, a preview of what was to come.

These people in the wilderness who saw God patient as a loving parent teaching his child to walk—holding those little hands to steady the pace over the rough places; patient as grandparents waiting through ten children playing a medley of "The Happy Farmer" before their grandchild does his recital piece; and patiently leading his redeemed people to the land ready for the taking by children grown up to the maturity of faith. These people took that brazen serpent Nebustan, with them through all their wanderings and turnings and claimings of their land, and in time they began to worship the bronze serpent instead of God. Years went by, kingdoms came and went, until one good king named Hezekiah tore down the bronze serpent Nebustan. He tore it down because he, Hezekiah, trusted in God and not the token that should have been left behind in the wilderness.

Sometimes God is silent to our listening hearts because we have a token, a talisman, an out-of-date pattern standing in the place where God and God alone needs to be. I think maybe the Nebustan fulfilled its purpose in the wilderness and had no purpose in the promised land. I think maybe the Nebustan was to be a preview of Christ, high and lifted up, bearing our sins on the cross that we might be forgiven, redeemed, set free of snakebite forever. I think maybe the Nebustan was a pattern for truth realized in maturity; and when we hold it too close and worship it, we never get to the robes of righteousness it represents. We are to grow up in all respects and lay childish things aside.

The apostle Paul had a glorious history. He was a protégé of the great Gamaliel. His ancestry could be clearly traced all the way back to the origin of the tribe of Benjamin. He was Pharisee of the Pharisees, according to the Law found to be blameless. What a future he had before him. What a story his life could have been. What a prestigious position he could have filled. But Paul said he was willing not only to give up all that to be found in Christ, but he called all that he lost garbage compared with what he gained in Christ.

Garbage? A position of the highest rank in the courts of the Pharisees counted as rubbish compared to the privilege of living hounded and hunted by his fellow man, squashed down into a basket and let down over a wall to escape death, imprisoned so many times that when he traveled he never bothered looking at the fancy tourist hotels' brochures but inquired about the conditions of the local prison where he probably would be staying. Garbage? Yes, anything that separates anyone from God is garbage, even a bronze statue that had had its day in the wilderness but is worthless in the land of Canaan.

Could it be that in the silence of God we need to put away childish things? Could it be that in our youth-oriented generation we have failed to exemplify the joys of maturity and have to deal with the highest suicide rate among young people that has ever been recorded? Could it be that regrets and unrealized ambitions stand between us and fellowship with the Most High God? I don't know. That's rough talk for an adult who wanted more than anything else in the world to be a famous actress, who thought her name in lights on Broadway would be the ultimate joy. Called garbage? Yes. Not because it is wrong. Not because it would not be right for someone else. Not because it was not a lovely goal but because God had something else in mind. Something that would take the training and technique designed for the satisfaction of stardom and use it for different stars.

And if in a wayward moment of weariness in the job assigned, or in the looking back with a misspent sigh, the Nebustan taunts you or me or Paul the gallant apostle, it's high time to call it garbage, and to clear the eyes for worship and the ears for small talk with the God of largess.

Dear Lord,

I want to extract the precious from the worthless, just as you have said. But dear Lord, I'm not sure I can tell the difference. It seems too much responsibility for me to know what to throw away and what to keep. I'm constantly measuring one against the other. What seems good in my sight may be ready for the garbage in yours, and what I might throw away as waste could easily be treasure to you. I'm stuck in some horrible phase of obedience. I can't do anything for fear of doing the wrong thing.

Could you just sketch it out in the clouds or maybe make an announcement from a loud speaker, "Throw away," and I'll do that; "Keep this," and I'll do that? Could it be you are teaching me in small beginnings so that I will learn your values and trust you in the bigger dilemmas of life?

Maybe this is faith. Maybe I have come to the divine junction where faith and reasoning find a common answer. Where I make my peace with the fact that you are God and I am not. I want to do the right thing. And you have said you will honor that with your dedication.

Dear Lord, guide my hands, direct my mind, and fill my heart that within all the keeping and letting go I learn to recognize what is precious in your sight. And thank you, Lord, that as I begin to throw out what I think clutters my life, the garbage man does not come every day. What is thrown away by error today, I may be able to reclaim by obedience tomorrow.

Amen.

CHAPTER 14

Whose Line Is It Anyway?

My husband and my friend Sissy picked me up at the airport. Leaving the airport for home, we plunged into the swimming pool of a thunderous rain. Lightning, swirling waters overflowing the street, darkness challenging the car's headlights as drivers cautiously made their way through the traffic. I was in the backseat amidst my luggage and waves of guilt for having brought my husband and friend into such a storm. I apologized, "I'm so sorry to get you out in this. I'm so sorry to cause you this much trouble." My apologies continued without the grace of variety.

As we turned into the freeway progressing slowly toward home, my husband, in the front passenger seat, turned his attention to my moaning monologue of contrition. "Jeannette," he said (departing momentarily from his usual "Honey"),

"Jeannette, I'm going to tell you something that will surprise you." My attention diverted momentarily, I listened intently for the surprise. "Jeannette," he continued, "you are not in charge of the weather." The storm abated gradually, and in its wake I had a new principle for abundant living within the silences of God.

Check carefully to see if you have picked up an assignment that is not yours. I am not in charge of the weather, and when I focus my energy on such false administrative details, I get no direction from God. The directions come in the packaging of the assignment and are not tossed about in the winds of chance or spread out for the newest whomever, like a counter cluttered with unclaimed items from the postal service. God will answer your willingness with an assignment specifically designed for your capacity. That capacity is a gift from God that he either gave you, is now giving you, or will give you as soon as you stop laboring over someone else's job and clear the deck for yours. The gift of help does not call us to usurp someone else's job but to stand ready to help that someone do his job better by doing our job well.

In our theater we have many different jobs. The fellowship of the team involves us in a communal viewpoint but does not thrive when any of its members is attending to a task not within his working assignment. Awareness of need may be a plea for considerate attention, but awareness of need does not necessarily constitute a call.

God, who is infinitely and intimately involved in every aspect of his child's life adventure, grants proper equipment for any of his assignments but does not burden any of us with detailed instructions for assignments he has not detailed for us. Once during an exciting football game, a player on the bench followed a play with such enthusiasm that as the opposing team rushed toward a touchdown, he—the player on the bench—burst out on the field to tackle the football-carrying runner. The player jumping from the bench expressed commendable support for his team; he exhibited an honorable spirit of involvement. However, the assignment of muscular participation was not his.

I have a friend who lovingly responds to any question, whether or not it is asked of her. If she overhears someone asking for information, the fact that the question is not directed to her or relevant to her abilities in no way deters her enthusiastic response. As a result, errors are distributed like shopping coupons and, most significantly, the specific direction of God seems to be missing. Sometimes the silence of God comes from confusing the labels on the assignments of God. The need for discernment in this complex issue takes the full strategy of prayer and occasionally the help of counseling in the fine art of label reading. Remember, he never asks the cobbler to bake his bread or the baker to mend his shoes although both the cobbler and the baker may be newcomers to the assignment.

Every principle has its inherent exceptions. Most certainly this one does. Every missionary, every family member, every team player, every hardworking administrator, knows there are times when the commands of workers don't match the demands of the work. Someone underequipped has to hold the ground until the equipped gets there, and sometimes the equipped don't get there at all. Well, to coin a phrase, that's show business.

The show must go on, with one terrified understudy clutching her script, or one shaky stage manager fumbling with the cues, or even one stammering volunteer introducing the main speaker when she did not know his name, his topic, or which of the prominent guests seated at the head table he was. I have done all three and done them badly, but someone had to do it and I did. But the exceptions don't dismiss the principle. In the silence of God, check to see if you have picked up somebody else's assignment.

God in his sovereign wisdom frequently assigns us to jobs not listed among our favorite choices. That is his prerogative. Also, in favoring the out-of-line football player, a world of smiling standbys never gets the work done, and in my humble opinion the errant player from the bench is better than the assigned tackler who missed his job. And in the matter of weather, God is not likely to share his authority, even with forecasters who often suffer from the falsely assigned responsibility. Occasionally, the silence of God is a good time to check God's agenda sheet. We may be called to cheer and not to chore.

In the silence of God, be assured his silence does not mean he is inactive. God has the right to his mysteries, and God has the right to his silences. Even I, given to much talking, have the right to my silences. There are times when I fail to appreciate that right in the silences of others and will take silence as a sign of disinterest when it is merely a thoughtful punctuation. As a theater veteran I know that silences are as necessary to meaningful dialogue as words spoken. All this I know, and yet when God is silent, I wonder if he is distant from me, disinterested in or dissatisfied with me. I need to be reminded that the silence of God does not necessarily mirror the inactivity of God. God is at work, even between his spoken words.

Years before I needed it, a soft-voiced Sunday school teacher gave me a principle for living in the silences of God. Her name was Grace Green, and the principle was rich with grace. The story of Joseph and his dispassionate brothers is a great tale of the storied patriarchs of biblical history. Joseph had a dream of God's specific calling of Joseph to leadership. The dream was for Joseph; the sharing of it with his brothers was Joseph's idea, and apparently the brothers did not enjoy hearing of Joseph's excellence, got tired of his being the favorite, and decided to get rid of him. So they hid him in a pit. His deliverance from the pit was brought to pass by the passing of a caravan on its way to Egypt. Grace Green's principle was the happy truth that the caravan had started its mission months before Joseph had his sorry pit stop. God's deliverance was well on its way before his child prayed for help. Remember that in the silent pit of despair, of despondency of defeat, God's caravan is already on its way!

As for the pit, it can be dirty, grimy, smelly, awful. A pit is a pit. And it can resound with the apparent silence of God. Quick comments on how to survive in the pit:

1. Don't unpack. Don't settle down in the pit. Believer, you may have parked your cell phone, pocket radio, and paperback novel on the landing above you, but the pit is not your home. The devil loves to convince you that you will never again see daylight, the nightly news, or your grandchild's piano recital—but do not establish residence in the pit. You are in transit.

2. Please don't decorate the pit. Pits are pits! There may be good in them which you will savor after you get out, but

don't lie to your senses by trying to make the walls of despair attractive. Painting windows and fluttering curtains may give your sodden talents exercise, but it also may lull your senses into thinking the pit will win the holiday contest for the best decoration of the neighborhood. Don't decorate!

3. Major principle—don't lock the door. Be sure you are open to the love of Christ who enters the pit to get you out. Under enormous stress I have learned one of the grandest truths in the Christian adventure: in despair, defeat, crushing sorrow, or bitter loss, never, ever, ever separate yourself from the community of believers. Depression's worst play for continuance is isolation. Don't lock yourself in. Don't lock deliverance out. The metaphor of a pit rarely houses the little church in the wildwood, but get yourself to the church on time. Drag yourself to community worship services. Your clothes may be grimy with pit stains; your shoes may be cloggy with mire. It may even be possible that some worshippers fail to welcome you properly in your condition, and the top row of the second balcony may be the only open seating, but take it as yours and connect with the community of faith. Seek a community of faith that honors Christ. There are imitations that may be even worse than the pit. The community of true faith will be a lifeline. A recent experience of suffering disenabled me from my customary manner of hope. My pit had neither sun nor moon nor distant star, but my community of faith got to me. It swarmed in upon me and literally kept me on the line of communication with the living God.

4. Listen for God. He makes pit stops. Your heart may not hear him, but your ears can. Talk to yourself about him. Tell

yourself stories from your childhood of faith. Keep the channel open. I have said and have heard from others the pitiful phrase, "But none of that matters anymore." So what. Don't wait for the matter to matter; keep the moment in gear. In the concentration camp Corrie ten Boom used to recite recipes just to remind her of life. You can't cook in a pit, but you can remember the cooking. You may have lost your momentum, your manners, and the means, but even in the deepest pit, you've got choices. Choose to listen for God.

The caravan of deliverance is on its way, so live in the pit ready to leave it.

Memo

Living in New York City as a frequently unemployed actress, I was delighted by a thrift shop in my neighborhood. From that shop one could purchase designer dresses that may have been worn only a few times by the rich and famous. One afternoon I was planning ahead for being taken that night to the opening of a major Broadway show. Hoping to look like a major Broadway actress, I dashed to the thrift shop and bought a black jumper with a red designer label.

That evening, I dressed happily. Under the black jumper was a bright sweater, and with a scarf draped carefully, I looked sufficiently jazzy to enter the opening night event with ease. My date commented favorably on my looks and the fact that I was on time, and we went to the theater.

As we settled into our seats, I glanced at the lady of the couple beside us. She was dressed in my black jumper! And then I realized mine was not a jumper. It was an elegant low-cut dress. The lady had added one sparkling diamond to her bulging bust line, and there I sat, turtlenecked to my chin with a silver feather pin I had had in college without a snitch of diamond. My self-confidence drained away. My ease was a thing of the past. My attire was a comment on my naive and unfashionable view of style.

Then I realized three things: (1) No one with or without glasses would ever recognize my tailored jumper as the other lady's vampy, high-couture attire. (2) I wouldn't look like the lady even without the turtleneck sweater. (3) If I spent the evening worried about my looks, I would not enjoy the show. So I had a good time and enjoyed the show while the breast-heaving lady's escort went to sleep and the two of them left at the first intermission.

Principle: another person's costume has little to do with yours, and self-worth is not won by comparison but by completeness. So, seek ye first the completeness of Jesus, and let the neckline fall where it may.

CHAPTER 15

In the Center Ring

Once upon a time, when I was a little girl, my mother took me to the circus. It was a wonderful event crowded into a big tent with three rings of marvelous things happening. I can remember the wonder of the lights and beautiful ladies floating in the air, high above the wires and lacings. I remember the music and the marching of the elephants around the ring and that the lady looking like the top of my mother's powder jar waved at me. It was so fine.

Suddenly, one section of the tent fell in. It was to the right of us, and I remember the shouting and the scurrying of parents pulling their children away from the tumbling tent. My mother stood to look toward the fallen tent and must have put her arm around me. I can remember the feeling of her bringing me closer to her. And then there was silence. Shock that something so much a part of wonderment would suddenly entrap part of its audience. At first silence, and then there were screams from inside the fallen tent. Muffled screams and high-pitched sobs of crying.

I was young, maybe six or seven, and I can't remember all the details clearly, but what I remember is as fresh as yesterday. One elephant was brought in with an attendant running beside him. Joining the elephants circling the ring, he became their leader and got them out of the arena. A lady aerialist, seated on a swinging bar, continued swinging while two on the high wire returned to the bases. I noticed the spotter on the ground signaling directions to those in the air. After that first beat of silence, everything I heard happened at once, like some encompassing circus sound system that lost the distinction of its acts. The thumping of the canvas, the cries from those engulfed, strains of calliope music that had no connection with what was happening, the rhythm of the elephants' march and one's trumpeted cry mixed with the shouts of their trainer. From the loud-speaker spoken words, unintelligible, punctuated all that I heard. The circus was still active, but the main event was the collapsed canvas covering those who, in one split second, had become victims.

And then the clowns rushed in. From every entrance to the arena, it seemed like an army of them. The first of them rushed to the section enveloped by the tent, lifted the covering, and went inside the folds of the tent. They went inside to bring out children and worried parents. These clowns, made up and costumed as entertainers, became heroes. And another section of clowns rushed to our area and entertained us. They did their comic tumbling and balanced balloons, and one had a little black dog that did tricks. One who had two puppet creatures in his hands came up the aisles and talked with the children. We laughed with them and talked with them, but I kept glancing at what was happening under the fallen tent.

If I remember correctly, one of the poles holding that section of canvas had snapped, and several rows of audience were covered by the heavy tent tarpaulin. No one was seriously hurt. Several parents left with crying children, and a circus manager directed the lifting of the twisted pole, and someone seemed to be collecting information. The circus resumed its programming after an announcement from the ringmaster, but I kept thinking of that section of audience who, while enjoying the circus, had been suddenly engulfed by an overpowering tent.

I remember the clowns. So many of them and how quickly they came, even before the elephants had made their way out of the ring, while the white-suited figures in the air were still balancing their way back to pole positions, before the audience changed their seats, there were the clowns.

Recently my tent fell in. I was enveloped, trapped, and overwhelmed.

My husband died.

This wonderful man who, in spite of weakenings and limitings and lessenings, had loved me vigorously, and I loved him with all my heart. He was in a nursing home after a series of strokes, but he was seldom less than himself and vitally interested in the people and active details of the life he had so actively lived.

We had just been to our doctor whose wise support had been a godsend. The doctor's opinion was that we would soon get my husband home. I went to New York for a business meeting. The two days before I left had been wonderful. Lorraine had been to his office, which he visited one day a week, and sat outside in the sunshine while friends came by for an unplanned gathering around this loved gentleman who, from his wheelchair, hosted the world. The day before I left, Lorraine was in great spirits, and we enjoyed our time together while talking about my next day's trip.

The next day I was called by the nursing home because they thought he had a fever, but they could not find a thermometer on the nursing floor. From New York I called the management to arrange for a thermometer. During his illness we had had wonderfully attentive caregivers and a few who had no care to give. When a thermometer was found, there was some question as to how it could be read. But the nurse assured me the condition was something that could be taken care of without hospital attention. I was unable to get a flight home until later the next day. His condition worsened, and he was in the hospital emergency room when I got to him. And then he died from a bacterial infection that had moved with vicious rapidity. The situation would have been the same had I been there or had a thermometer been available, but both absences continue to taunt me with the foolish rhetoric of what might have been.

My husband died.

In an instant I became part of the multitude who know experientially the details of such loss—the shock that causes grief to hold its breath, the timid exploring of being alone, the onslaught of matters (all critical) that must be handled immediately, the determined transition from *is* to *was*, and the immediate draining away of order. No amount of planning, discernment, or intellect stems the draining away of order. Like leftover tub water disappearing with its bubbles down the drain, order left my life because the single support of its procedure was gone. My tent collapsed, and I was overwhelmed.

I continued breathing, but I was not sure why. My thinking pattern had blanks where there had been words and names and intentions. From my home I heard, as for the first time, the traffic pattern from distant streets simply because in my life there was nothing else to hear.

It was not an unnatural thing that had happened. Death is itself a natural thing, an experience common to all created beings. I had been by its side before—my father, my mother, my friends, my coworkers. I knew the path to the funeral home, but this was different.

My husband died.

I was overwhelmed. My tent fell in. And where were the clowns? And so, they came. The clowns. Holy clowns. Angelic clowns. Focused clowns. A veritable sainthood of clowns—the community of faith. The believers, the family of God. And I who had no children, no brothers, no sisters—I, drowning in the current of loss, was rescued by a family who, taking orders from the holy parent, knew exactly what to do.

They came individually, and they came in swarms. A team took over my house and fed people I didn't recognize with food I didn't know how to prepare. There was someone spending the night on a downstairs sofa. There was someone to drive me, someone to go with me to choose the casket, someone to answer the telephone, someone to call a hasty list notifying them of the death, someone to sing at the service. There were lines of someones at the visitation. There were someones at the burial. There was someone to call me the next morning. I was never alone; there was always someone with me.

And there was someone gone.

God marshaled a team who came into my fallen tent to comfort, to conduct, and to console. Other friends joined this team. From years of working with Lorraine came men and women who knew their loss and comforted mine. Thousands of letters and cards came and continued to come as the news seeped through the patterns of busy lives. There were people who wanted to entertain me, people who wanted to cheer me, people who climbed under my fallen tent to be with me. Grief has its own personality. I doubt that any two people grieve exactly the same. And comfort has its own personality. Individuals help in individual ways and at individual times.

With the first wave of comforters, I learned—and immediately—what stupid things I had been saying to my grieving friends. When I sensed the pattern of statements bounce off my dim-hearing ears, I recognized my errors when I had tried to comfort. I remembered that even in those ineffective words I had offered others, even in their inappropriate syllables, I had loved and wanted to help. Realizing that, I made a significant decision: to hear everything said as love. I believe it must have been the prompting of God. Everything said to me, I heard as love, and everything said helped.

I learned I had a small battle with the thought of so much being done for me. The evening my house was filled with helpers, I turned to Deborah, my friend and assistant, and said,

"What do I do for them?" All those people in my house were guests, and I needed to be the hostess, but I couldn't remember where the party napkins were. A couple turned over to me a room in their home near the emergency room of the hospital, and I thought, *What can I do in return for their hospitality?* A friend drove down from Dallas just to be with me, and I worried over what I could do for her who had done so much for me? The listing went on and on, and I added fretfulness to my already full agenda. Finally I began to learn a major discipline: it is not always more blessed to give than to receive. Occasionally it is more blessed to receive, and that was difficult for me.

Grace is a heavy gift. Its assignment is reception. I have often thought that one of the noblest things Jesus did was to receive from those to whom he came to give. My own offering to him was small in my hands, but when he received it, it became large in significance. The little tin tray with copper handles that I made in my craft class at youth camp was nothing in my hands, but when my mother received it and put it on her dressing table, it became a work of art. The butternut squash filled with peanut butter and ginger was an awkward attempt at creative cooking, but when my husband received it and asked for a second helping, it became a culinary masterpiece. When I came to Jesus, I was a stammering mixture of apology and errors, but when he received me, I became a treasure of royalty.

In the crisis of need, be receptive. Let the clowns serve you, and determine to hear anything they say as love.

Most importantly, in the crisis or out of the crisis, stay close to the believing community. People of all faiths helped me then and help me now. I have many friends who are not believers, and I love them and am grateful for their friendship and affection. I believe Jesus Christ is the only way and that there is no other name under heaven given among men whereby one must be saved. I believe that completely, but I also believe the carefulness of help given is to be received with grace even if not given in it. But oh, the shower of graciousness spilling all over my needs was received with great gratitude.

And in all of this, God was silent.

I read every Scripture I was offered. At the service for my husband, the preacher's words were so deeply personal in their honoring that I celebrated each syllable in my ears and in my heart. My friends and my family, and Lorraine's family and his coworkers and those to whom he had been a role model, and the community we had shared spoke accurately to me, and I found enormous strength coming from them.

But in all of this, God was silent.

I heard philosophies and phrases and felt their wisdom standing by me for such a time when I might more deeply consider them. I was welcomed into hope by those who had preceded me in the experience of loss. I knew my husband's faith, and remembering that was the finest of oils to my dry heart. I yearned to hear his voice and regretted I had never recorded him. I slept with one of his sweaters between the pillow and my tears. I went back to work quickly and scraped up narrow sidings of energy that didn't quite work but held the place for those that might be filling later. I tried to answer all the gifts and sharings and offerings of caring.

And in all of this, God was silent.

And I found that silence strangely compatible. Words were not needed. I didn't have to say them, and neither did God. Through all those days that seemed to be endless and really were, I learned many things about the silence of God.

Cleaning my husband's shower, I suddenly became angry. My husband had built our house but lived in it only a year before his illness. He had designed that shower with special care and had had such a short time using it. I cried out loud to God, "That is not fair!" I waited for the thunder of punishment, for the shaking of sovereign rebuke. There was none. For God was silent.

In the silence I realized I had not said or felt anything against God. It was the situation that I addressed. In my limited understanding, it was unfair.

And I leaned my head against the shower door and wept aloud. There was no one to hear me, no one to try to hush my weeping, no one to tell me to be brave or think on the bright side or even to finish cleaning the shower. There wasn't a Bible verse or a prayer or a shadowing of angel wings.

There was only me and my silent God, and that was more than enough.

And then one early morning when I was crying, I reckoned deeply with the honor of my tears. I was weeping in the absence of a man who left nothing behind him but the echoes of his worthiness. He was a strict leader who left no doubt about his authority but treated even those who opposed him with such respect that neither his winnings nor his losings left a trail of bitterness. We were two very different people. We took different stands on many issues. Our life together was far too lively to be always in agreement. But there was never an argument that separated us; the arguments kindled the fires of our individuality, and each of us honored the individuality of the other. We laughed a lot with each other and at each other. I could easily say:

This man I loved was gentle and kind.

He changed my world and never changed his mind.

He was a man of great integrity. Almost every one of the letters written to me about him used that phrase, "a man of great integrity."

And suddenly, in that early morning, I was overcome by a surging, waving, encompassing gratitude. I was grateful that I had known the joy while I was in it. Lorraine and I spoke of it and thanked the Lord together. We knew we had something wonderful when we had it. I had no regrets of unrecognized appreciation. That morning there was no lifting of sorrow, no final trumpet to closing grief, no easing of the situations that confounded me; but there was sweeping, cleansing, glorifying-to-God gladness. And I said aloud, tears crowding one another down my cheeks, "Oh God, thank you!"

And God spoke and said, "You're welcome."

He had never left me. He kept all his promises. He would somehow guide me through the abyss that was now an uninviting future. He would let me weep and grieve and live through the valley of the shadow of death without trying to pretend it was a garden in the sunshine.

You don't have to make up a voice of God when you don't hear one. He hates imitations and said so. You don't have to apologize if you hear his voice and others do not or belabor yourself when others hear his voice and you do not. You really don't have to do any of it, but stay close to the community of faith. That community may translate the silence of God into hearable sentences. Don't forsake the written Word. He makes his deposits from it that you can cash in on later.

Do hear love, no matter how it is expressed. Do take your own time walking through the valley. It has flowers of its own that never bloom anywhere else. Do know that grief has a beginning, a middle, and an end. All of it is hard, and none of it is wasted. Do know that the silence of God never limits him, so never let it limit you.

The funeral was a gathering of many people. I was touched by the numbers that came remembering my husband with personal interaction. Everyone talked to me with such personal involvement in the loss.

But God was silent.

I prayed fervently for God's direction, for his nudging of me into the right answers. I believe now and believed then that God was caring for me, but he was silent.

On the way from the church to the cemetery, our caravan of cars needed extra police escorts, and those men came and handled the intricate matter of traffic well. I was impressed by their professionalism in directing traffic away from our car-to-car route. Family members joined me in the limousine. We pulled out into traffic, and the police escort opened a way for us as we turned toward the freeway. We were a lengthy parade, and the escorts faced many challenges. Interstate 10 was heavily busy, car to car. One police escort halted the cars coming into I-10 as we drove past, and another signaled heavy vans to pull over to the side to make way for us. I-10 was open to us as cars were sent back, held back, and pushed to the edges of the free-way. And so the funeral procession for Lorraine George moved rapidly along I-10, the freeway open to us.

And my husband, Mr. Lorraine George, had built I-10. That section of the freeway over which we drove had been at one time a sketched out graphic in my husband's office, and now it was a highway for the builder.

And in my car I cheered.

And God was not silent.

Memo

Memory is a river, a flowing river. Sometimes it over-flows its banks, and its tears wash away edges of our land. With too much storming, it overtakes houses and gardens, and even the mightiest of trees tremble in its wake. There are times when its roaring is so fierce the dams of choice and reason lose their stance. I think the saddest times of memory are when it runs dry and what had been a flowing rushing of water is just brown tracing in an arid land. But in all its ways, it moves.

Regret is not a river; it is a stagnant pool. There's no fresh way in and no fresh way out, and in its dank stillness there is no produce. The things that live there are musty and mawkish, like fetid mandrakes that strangle any green or growing thing. Respect the flow of memories, but beware the swamp of regret.

There are three good reasons for looking back:

1. To learn from errors.
2. To gain compassion for others.
3. To laugh! If for no reason other than
laughter, which in itself is healing.

Regret accomplishes none of those. If tempted by its invitation, remember one grand and solid truth: What might have been never was. Don't take notes from its lectures, keep picture postcards of its shores, or schedule its tours. God will gladly rescue you from its banks, but he does not live there, vacation there, or advertise its lots.

CHAPTER 16

Surprise Celebration

My husband's first wife, Johnny, was a brilliant actress and director, and I performed in a couple of plays under her direction while she was on staff at Houston's Alley Theatre. Later she established a music theater in Houston that, until her death, was prominent in Houston's growing theater community. Lorraine's sister, Tony, was married to Bill Hardy, an actor and director who was with me in the Alley Theatre's acting company, and through that connection I got to know Lorraine. That casual connection was greatly encouraged by Tony, and Lorraine began to attend a Bible class I was teaching. Lorraine has said that he went to a Bible class and liked the Book so much he married the teacher.

In actuality the romance was not that simple. Lorraine became involved in all the areas of my life. He arranged dinner for me between the Saturday shows at the theater, regularly attended all my Bible classes, escorted my mother, with his mother, to the theater, and privately gained entrance into my apartment to surprise me with a lighted Christmas tree, set up and twinkling at me, when I came home from the theater. I realized this soft-spoken, unassuming man was becoming important in my life, and I found that to be a problem.

I explained to the Lord that I was content with my life. I had a full-time theater career, was directing a Christian theater, and was going about doing good and teaching Bible classes. I had no time for marriage. God was silent. My mother was not.

Seeing Lorraine's increasing attentions to me alerted my mother, and she did not like him. She called him "that man" and was horrified when, thinking he was helping her, he built her a new driveway. She called me to tell me "that man" was tearing up her backyard and she doubted he had ever done that kind of work before "in public." I told her he had built the parking lot for Houston's Sports Center, the first triple highway overpass in Houston, the underground system that brought water from Houston to Galveston, and all of that had been done "in public," but it did not comfort her.

I was also not comforted by his attentions and the fact that I found great joy in his attentions. Although Lorraine was one of the gentlest men I had ever known and supportive of what I did, I felt I was losing control of my life's plans. I earnestly prayed about this increasing problem, and God was silent.

My father had died several years before, and Lorraine had the audacity to tell my mother that he wanted to marry me.

She took to her bed for two days and wouldn't speak to either of us. Now neither God nor my mother was speaking to me.

I did not want to bring Lorraine into the conversations with my friends, who were already inviting him to church socials with me and remarking how interesting it was that Lorraine and I both liked buttermilk and he was so support-ive of theater. I continued to pray earnestly. I alerted God to the fact that I had accepted as from him the ministry of the A.D. Players and that this curly-haired, blue-eyed man with the lopsided grin, who made me feel like a princess or someone who had just won three Academy Awards, was distracting me from my mission. God was silent.

I had a break between rehearsals and performance, and I flew to Dallas to have some time to myself. I thought the problem was serious, and asked a strong, praying Christian friend of mine, Elsa Billman, to pray with me, for me, and about me. She did, I did, and God was silent.

I returned to Houston and told Lorraine that I couldn't marry him because my mother would never speak to me again, and besides I had all these things to do that had to do with Christian commitment. Lorraine said we needed to pray about it, it would be just fine with my mother, and he would see to it that I would serve my commitment better married to him than not married to him, and besides we needed to talk about when to have the wedding.

Lorraine left town, and while he was gone, I prayed with all my heart and tears. I told God that I wanted to do what he wanted me to do, but that I knew I loved this man who seemed to love me because he was putting up with me being difficult. I thanked God for putting Lorraine in my life and for having his sister arranging things so we could sit together, and having my friends like him, and I wanted to marry him, and I thought Lorraine was a wonderful gift for which I would thank the Lord all my life.

God was no longer silent.

My mother loved the wedding idea when we told her we wanted to get married on her wedding anniversary. Because when we said that, my mother knew she would not be left out, and all she really wanted was to be part of our story. We had a lovely wedding and an awesome marriage.

I realized that all the time I thought God was silent was because what I wanted with all my heart was what God had wanted for me, with his best intentions, and he had nothing else to say about it.

It's not a rule or principle that will fit with every desire or earnest yearning, but there are times when God's plans match the desires of our heart. And we are so determined to obey his holy no that we can't even hear his holy yes. Our ways are not God's ways, but sometimes God loves to put his way into our ways and wait in silence until we catch on.

In the silence of God, look for the gift. It might be just what you wanted.

Years ago, I used to do small programs for various groups. One such event was in a lovely home, and as I arrived, I saw the cars serviced by valet parking. The attendant took my car, and thanking him, I hurried up the walkway carrying my notes and small props under my arm. The door opened, and I introduced myself to the lady greeting me, and she ushered me into the room where coffee and various delicacies were being served. I glanced into the room where some of the guests were already seated and estimated the area I could use for my program. I told the lady at the door that I had another program scheduled in about an hour and would appreciate being able to present my small performance as soon as possible. She asked me what I needed, and I said I needed nothing but a little space, and if the ladies could sit around the piano, I would be able to work there. I went to get coffee, and she collected the ladies from outside in the garden and in the various rooms.

As soon as they settled, I did my program, which they received kindly, but without much enthusiasm. They were very quiet. I added to my planned presentation, hoping to gain interest, but earned only polite attention, so I concluded with a few words of thanks and left for the door. I had not met the hostess with whom the program had been arranged and said to the same lady who had originally welcomed me, "Please tell Mrs. McIntyre that I'm sorry I didn't get to meet her," and politely subtle, I said, "She can mail the honorarium to me whenever it's convenient." The lady nodded and said, "And who is Mrs. McIntyre?" I said, "The Mrs. McIntyre who is in charge of this club meeting." The lady at the door said, "This isn't a club meeting. My neighbor and I were having friends over for tea." I had come into the wrong house, arranged for the guests to assemble around the piano, and presented an unwanted program to a group of ladies for whom my topic made no sense! As it turned out, each of the hostesses thought the other must have arranged a program.

I was so embarrassed I did not recover sufficiently when I got to the house where I was expected but for whom I was very late. God had been disturbingly silent.

In the silence of God, check to see if you are depending on the appropriate audience.

After the death of my husband, I went immediately back to work. It was the right thing to do. In fact, I think we generally do the right thing to do in such circumstances, even though the right thing may not assure us of its rightness. I regret several of my choices, but looking back honestly, I estimate that with the information I had at the time, I was making a right choice. Given the same circumstances and knowing what I know now, I would have done differently, but at the time of the choice and with the information I had at that time, I did about as well as I could.

I like doing what I do and found in it some satisfaction that pleased me deeply. I also found in it some dissatisfaction. The work done wholeheartedly did not wholeheartedly assure me. I tried to correct it, to rearrange it, to shape it, to demand of it what I needed from it, and it did not work. And God was silent.

I did not recognize it, but I was depending on an inappropriate audience. I was expecting the work and its workers to meet the new needs I had. I was doing the same thing I had done gathering strangers around the piano in that lovely home and expecting the wrong audience to feed back the right response. Instruments in the orchestra can only bring to the music that which they are equipped to bring. Frustration is the result of doing the same wrong thing over and over again, expecting the right response.

Years ago, after a rehearsal, two of the company's actors were out in a pouring rain trying to fix a tire. One of them, Tim Wathen, is still a good and supportive friend and loves to tell this story on me. I drove out into the street and saw the two young men in the driving rain, working at their problem. I wanted to help, so I drove to the corner grocery store and bought them a package of cookies. In a pouring down rain, cookies are at best only a soggy interruption and do absolutely nothing for the changing of a tire. There's nothing wrong with cookies. They were, in fact, oatmeal and raisin, my favorites. But they were inappropriate to the crisis. My intentions were good, but no degree of good intentions will meet the needs of two young men in the dark during a storm, trying to change a tire.

The work that I do may occupy me and give me a sense of active involvement in the ongoing pattern of life sprung out of shape by my grief, but to expect it and its people to fill up the canyon of hurt is a grave mistake, and the silence of God deepens its sorrow.

I stammer a bit at the unreasonableness of my suggestion in such a situation. Have a party.

Yes, have a party. In the appropriate time, not too early and not too late. Call in your friends. Friends that have some history to them. Friends who not only know and respect your loss but also participate in it as theirs. Allow them to add their memories to yours. Allow the laughter; it will not be rancid with mockery. Let the wine of love, tried in the fire of time shared, bring you unapologetic joy.

Be sure the friends are true and not strangers to the table of sorrow. Let them be. Don't hover over them like a dove counting its nestlings. Let them be. You will find the merriment only temporary. Your grief or sorrow will be only briefly interrupted, and after the party you can pick up its pattern exactly where you left it. But somewhere in the party, during the naturalness of its merriment—not the awkwardness of false geniality—you will know God is not committed to silence forever and that neither are you.

If you have no such friends—and I grieve for you, for I have found my friends essential—plan the party anyway. Choose what you will wear. You may be bedded down with illness, but choose party clothes for your mind.

There is a strange and startling verse in the strange and startling book of Ecclesiastes. I found Ecclesiastes by accident. I was teaching a Bible class that had some time left over and said, "Why don't we zip through a study of Ecclesiastes?" I had not previously studied Ecclesiastes, and when I got into it, I said, "Oh Lord, if you ever get me out of Ecclesiastes, I'll never leave Philippians again!" But I found so much of the voice of God in Ecclesiastes that it has become one of my top ten favorite books.

Ecclesiastes doesn't mince words. It says out loud just how bad life can be. And it says with crackling reality just how good life can be when it is as bad as life can be. In the midst of listing all the griminess of life, Ecclesiastes says, to always wear white. Why in the world wear white? In the midst of all the oppression and sorrow and wastefulness and regretfulness, why wear white? Simply because white is the color for celebration. The somber songster of Ecclesiastes says: Never, ever, throw away your party clothes.

Psalm 137 is one of the saddest of the psalms. It is sung in the cadences of sorrow. Israel, that great and glorious nation is in captivity—away from their center of worship, away from their homeland, away from joy, and away from fellowship. They moaned by the rivers of Babylon and hung their harps upon the weeping willow trees because they thought they would never sing again. Never rejoice. Never delight. Never have a party. And they were wrong. God had a plan beyond even the disciplinary suffering. God never rebukes without the hope of restoration. He doesn't waste anything, not even discipline. But in the silence of God, his rebuked people thought the music was silenced forever, and their harps were wasted.

Pain can drown out the music—the hymns and the bagpipes, the songs and the jokes. Pain has a loud voice. And pain is to be respected. God respected it, why should we not? The cross is one ugly, awful, consummate exclamation mark affirming God's respect for pain. The nails were real, the stretching of the body was real, the blood was real, the sense of separation from God was real. God knows experientially all about pain. And the silence of God, like his grace, was beyond our understanding, but it was sufficient. Pain may give us a hint of understanding for the price he paid, and in that understanding we hear a whisper of how much worth we have in his sight. But pain in its dominance gets our full attention, and so it does for God.

Pain is not a joke. Pain is not a figment of imagination. Pain hurts. God knows that. I don't understand it, but I don't have to. Understanding pain is not its resolution. Knowing the name of the illness doesn't cure it. (Or we wouldn't have prescriptions and drug stores and commercials.) Where is God when its hurts? Somewhere in it and knowing it. Don't ask him why, just be glad he's there.

In the pain, in the sorrow, in the wanton wanderings of the grief-muffled mind, know in what closet you parked your party dress. Because, dear child of the living God, there is a party coming, and you are invited.

David, the psalmist king, cried out in sorrow, "I would have despaired had I not believed I would see the goodness of the Lord in the land of the living." It's in Psalm 27, and I love to read that song because David goes back and forth between jubilation and despair. Jubilation wins. David is saying life has its downs and downs, but my party clothes are ready for the party.

And so, I had a party. And my friends came. My party dress didn't fit because one of us had changed sizes, and I barely got to my party in time because I had crowded into my day too much of the work that hadn't worked for me. But I got to the party just in time. And my harp had gotten a little rusty on the willows, but that didn't matter because no one asked me to play it anyway. And I didn't have to bring any music; it came with my friends. God knew all the words, and he was not silent.

There are many reasons God is silent. Some you have to address, and some you have to accept. For the believer the silence of God is always temporary and is frequently interrupted by his love expressed through celebration, just when it seemed inappropriate and was really just in the nick of time.

Memo

As I was writing this book, due to the evil intentions of my computer, two chapters were lost—never to be reclaimed, never to come up again, never to be rescued. It was final and awful and a bad thing to have happened. After I cried, screamed, and tried desperately to find someone on whom I could blame the mishap, I gave up the chapters and settled down to write again.

And then an interesting thing happened. Those lost chapters became the best I had ever written. Those never-to-be-found words had brilliance beyond my highest expectations. The principles were clear, succinct, to the point, and properly spelled. In the glaring light of their excellence, I did not want to write again—ever! Those chapters had more authority over me than anything I could ever write. And God was silent.

Where were you, God, when I punched the wrong button and lost the finest contemporary literature? Where were you, God, when I was happily about my work and understandably fatigued by the concentrated efforts on your behalf and erased my very best? Why were you silent then and silent now? Are you lurking in the shadows of my remorse, ready to pounce on my broken spirit with evidence that the loss was my fault? Where were you then? Where are you now? And where would I be without you?

God had only one answer: I am God. I am here. I was then. I will be there. Where are you?

I never found the chapters I wrote, but I learned that God is not filed with what was lost. He is an ever-present verb and directs our attention to the moment, assured that he will be present in the future. If we stop asking where he was and start being where we are, where we are going is not so frightening.

In the silence, check your demands on the past. What has been said cannot be unsaid. What was done cannot be undone. Dismiss it! And the first miracle of his talking in the silence is that we are listening.

CHAPTER 17

Home Address

$\mathcal{I}$admit it. I have a secret. I have had it and kept it secret for many years. Few knew it. Now as a public speaker, I tell my secret often, hoping the telling will relieve it of its troubling authority, but it does not! I have told it to women's conferences, to management workshops, to drama workshops, to youth meetings, and once, through an interpreter, to a Christian Women's Club in Okinawa, Japan. Each time I have told it, there has been response. I have had men, women, young people, and senior citizens take me aside to tell me that my secret expressed helped them in the dilemma of the same secret. Established professionals, company executives, freshmen students, and graduate professors have shared their understanding of my secret. And this is my secret: I struggle with the need to belong, to fit in, to know I am welcomed.

When personality types are analyzed, I don't fit comfortably into any category. When workshops define gifts, mine lack definition. When I had my colors analyzed, the two assessors disagreed and left mad at each other.

I married late, and when I first went shopping for my wedding dress, I was shown dresses appropriate for the mother of the bride. When I first attended conferences for artistic directors of Christian theater companies, I was the only woman. When I first spoke on company management, I was the only one there who was in theater. When I was in the front line of professional theater, I was the only Christian in the company, and in my church I was the only representative of professional theater. Before I was born, I was named Hubert.

Maybe the women identify, because in this generation of defining womanhood (and generally incorrectly), we leave out many women who don't define easily. Maybe it's because the hardworking man, a purposeful executive, feels he is less than qualified to be husband and father. Maybe it's because we have not made clear that the longing for a place to belong is not a peculiar attribute and has an answer—and a good one.

Years ago I was to speak at a large drama conference in Louisville. Gregory Peck was to be the main speaker, Horton Foote was to direct a workshop, and I was to speak at the luncheon in between the major events. I had sprained my back and called the conference coordinator to cancel my appearance, but he was so eager to have me, he volunteered to have me met by ambulance and carried to my speaking time on a stretcher. I assured him I would be there without needing the critical care units and arrived with a cane, but on schedule, the morning of the meeting.

My hosts met my plane, and I was taken directly to the auditorium for Mr. Peck's opening address. I asked my hosts if I might miss that meeting, getting a little time to rest before my lunch-time speaking. The hosts did not answer immediately. Mr. Peck would not be speaking as he had a conflict in scheduling work on a movie. Mr. Foote could not cover for him as he had also had to cancel. The only replacement they had for Mr. Peck was me, and we were on our way to that meeting as I heard the news. Being Gregory Peck's replacement was news to me and news to the hundreds gathered in the auditorium to hear him. No one had been told of the adjustment, and as I walked with my host onto the stage and saw a large, crowded auditorium packed with people eager to hear Gregory Peck, I was— to say the least—fully aware I was not the one they expected.

I was once asked to cover, at the last minute, for an outstanding quarterback who was scheduled to address a large conference of the splendid Fellowship of Christian Athletes. At that event I told them my sports were jumping to conclusions and weight lifting—every time I stood up.

The question is, where do I fit in, how do I overcome the fact I am not the one everyone expected, and will I ever belong?

And the answer is Psalm 84:3; the flitting sparrow and fluttering swallow have found their place, and so have I. "But by God's grace I am what I am" (1 Cor. 15:10). By the grace of God through Jesus who is the Christ, I fit in, and I am exactly whom God expected. If I come to the Lord as Gregory Peck,

I hear nothing from God because what he wants to say to Gregory Peck he says to Gregory Peck. If I come to the Lord as an outstanding athlete, he has nothing to say to me because what he wants to say to an outstanding athlete he says to an outstanding athlete. If I come to the Lord as anyone but me, he has nothing to say to me because what he wants to say to anyone but me he says to anyone but me.

I have learned from experience and from Scripture that I must come to God as I am, not as whom I wish I were or whom I think I should be, or whom others think me to be. My right to be face-to-face with God is a result of Christ's offering himself on my behalf. To pick up the package of grace Christ bought for me, I have to come in the honesty of my needy self or the holy post office will not honor my claim check printed "Package ready to be delivered."

As a special gift from God, I belonged happily in my marriage. I had only been married a few years when I had the opportunity of doing *The Hiding Place* film. Working with Jimmy Collier, a brilliant director, and Julie Harris, one of the great actresses of our time, was a wonderful opportunity. After that film was completed and released, I was caught up in a whirlwind of events—public appearances, television interviews, sudden activities, and hobnobbing with names and personalities living in the limelight. Frequently I found myself wearing a name tag in the public eye that was not my own. The Christian community wanted me to be Corrie ten Boom. The secular community wanted me to be a movie star. I was neither. It was not easy to hold on to my own simple identity, but I had major help.

My husband never asked me for my autograph, never mistook me for Corrie, and thought the fact that I was a movie star was a pleasant amusement for us to enjoy together. He and I went to a showing of the film and I wanted to go into the theater as an ordinary member of the audience with popcorn and chocolate mints. We waited in line for tickets, and Lorraine suggested I tell them who I was to get seated conveniently. I refused, and so my husband and I, with the tickets he had paid for, stood with about thirty other standees in the back of the theater to see the film starring me. He never complained, but he did murmur, as we stood throughout the film, that he hoped the next film I did would be a shorter movie because being married to a movie star does not mean privileges.

Many friends who knew me before the movie and liked me then did not change their affection during the brief time I was a celebrity. And most importantly, God had welcomed me face-to-face long before my face was on a movie screen. He held me close, and with or without screen credits, I was exactly the one he expected.

Let me add a postscript to my secret.

Neither success nor failure is a remedy for the aches and pains of doubting one's personal value. Failure does not make it worse; it just makes it known. Insecurity is not dismissed by fame; it is deepened by it. Success does not heal the dilemma; it increases it. Doing something well does not alleviate self-doubts, and when the self-doubter is asked to repeat what was done well, the resultant terror is beyond description.

I once asked Eileen Heckart, that fabulous actress of worldwide fame, what was her greatest fear, knowing she is recognized as a great and successful actress. She thought a minute and then said, with her customary honesty, "The fear that someone will find out I'm really not that good." Aim high, do well, but don't expect success to settle the issue. That settling of selfhood is only found secured and discovered in the hand of God.

For years a major battle has been going on in my backyard. I have a small bird feeder that is there for the express purpose of feeding birds. Squirrels not only eat from it, but they settle into it and scare the birds away. I lecture the birds, telling them that each of them is equipped with a beak and claws and together they would be a match for any squirrel. They don't catch on to the power of their equipment and scatter like dandelions in the wind at the first approach of the squirrel. I have tried every-thing I could find. The hardware store had a special feeder that included a spring-loaded perch that would send the squirrels, chirping and wide-eyed, into the bushes below the feeder. The squirrels figured it out and would stand on the top of the feeder causing it to sway rapidly back and forth and scatter the seeds all over the ground. Then I bought a package of crystals that would keep the squirrels away. The crystals weren't crystals; they were chunks of fox manure and kept the birds, me, and the meter reader away. The squirrels got used to the smell before the rest of us did and returned to their former eating habits.

One morning I figured out the pathway the squirrels used to enter the bird feeder and their escape route when I, waving a mop, chased them out of the feeder. I stood statue-like and glared eye to eye with the first squirrel and then the second squirrel. It worked! After a while of my playing statue with mop in the driveway, one little bird flew near the feeder. He looked in and saw it was empty of squirrels, but hopped away onto a swaying branch. Two other birds joined him while I kept guard over the squirrels. I hoped the birds would at least snatch a little breakfast or early lunch while I stood by, but they never dared. And I wondered, *Can't they see me?* I had to be quiet to stare down the squirrels, but surely the birds knew I was on their side.

And I wondered, *How often have I missed the fact of great God Almighty standing on my behalf?* And because he was silent, I missed the certainty of his attention.

His eye is on the sparrow, and the swallow, and the squirrels.

And even in his silence, "those who know his name will trust him" (Psalm 9:10, author's paraphrase).

CHAPTER 18

And the Winner Is . . .

As an only child, I grew up in a small family of three. But each personality in that threesome was unique, and at times my small family seemed like a crowd. My mother was a beautiful, gifted Southern lady with a gentle spirit and a stalwart strength. If I remember correctly, she was never afraid of anything except a mousetrap—not the mouse, which we carefully dismissed from our pet canary's feeding dish—but the trap. Being from south Alabama, her never-changing accent got more mileage out of a vowel than any other accent I have ever heard. During hurricane storms my father would pace the floor, saying he had to stay awake in order to get his family to higher ground. I would stay awake terrified of the sounds of wind and rain drumming against my windows. And Mother, who could not get her family to bed in spite of the fact that we lived on "higher ground" in a two-story house, would go to the piano and play Chopin and Bach and hymns throughout the storm. That is why I always remember music when I'm scared.

My father traveled full-time, trying to scrape together enough income from the early scavenging days of the oil business. He worked in the fields and would come home in hip-high heavy boots caked with mud. As a child I was often ill and could measure the degree of illness by certain changes in my home. If Mother had a friend staying with her, I knew there was a degree of seriousness. If that friend were a nurse and the doctor frequently dropped in on me, I knew that degree was elevated. But if I could hear the preacher praying from the living room, I knew the crisis was major.

During one such major crisis, I remember lying feverish in my bed in the middle of the night when I heard my daddy calling my name. Raising myself weakly on one elbow, I could see him standing in our driveway, covered with the oil and clay of his work, unshaven and tired, but calling my name. He had driven all night from a distant field and until he saw me in the window, didn't know whether he still had a daughter to call by name. Of course I recovered, but I will never forget that moment when my daddy came from far away to call me by name. I think of that when I read in the Scripture that Jesus calls his sheep by name. I am not to him a number. I'm a name, and a pet name at that.

My daddy and I played endless games of checkers. He always won. My mother would take him aside and say, "Let her win. She tries so hard." But my daddy still contested me with full skill. Over and over we got out the checkerboard, and I never won. Until one afternoon in the late summer, we were at the checkerboard on the back porch. Daddy was a silent player, and I learned to think through every move, even if only to give him some challenge before he won. And on this afternoon I won! I could not believe it. I stared at the checkerboard to see what error I had made. And there were none. I won, and my daddy was silent. I looked up at him and saw tears on his face and a grin wider than our back porch. He hugged me in a jubilance that only Olympic winners ever know. He said, "You won!" He called for my mother, who came hurrying from the kitchen. "She won!" And I knew in an instant what I have remembered for a lifetime. In his silence he wanted me to win.

Life is not a game. And if it were, competing with God is not a good thing to do. But sometimes when God is silent, he is waiting for us to win. Waiting for us to trust the training, teaching, and tutoring of his strategy and claim the victory he planned for us to celebrate.

My daddy and I played many games of checkers after that. Sometimes I won, sometimes I lost, but I knew forever that my daddy wanted me to win and believed that I was a winner.

God never calls us to performance until he has first called us to rehearse. Sometimes the rehearsals go on so long we forget there will ever be performance. Sometimes the rehearsal is so hard we're not sure the performance will be worth it. But in all times the rehearsals process unto performance, and in all times the performance is worth it!

Trust God in the silence. He may be concentrating on your winning and waiting to celebrate it.

> He took me to the tallest hill.
> Its narrow ledge was high.
> I feared he brought me there to fall.
> He brought me there to fly.

CHAPTER 19

Some Ice Carvings Never Melt

*T*he silence is often chosen punctuation for God Almighty. Before he spoke a word and created the heavens and the earth, there was silence. And there are sounds of God's holy silence in our days and our nights. Times when God holds his breath not in the absence of thought but in honoring the inadequacy of one of his greatest creations—speech.

Silence is part of speech, and in a few significant instances speech is part of silence. And even God is mute in choosing which is better.

Before the word of his creation, there was silence; and long, long ago God again interrupted the silence with a word spoken to a Babylonian descendant of Noah's son Shem. That word was astonishing. It not only changed the man's place of residence; it made of him a nomad, which I personally think his wife must have questioned with each packing up and telling the neighbors where to send any mail or further angelic pronouncements that may have found it difficult to keep up with all the moves. I assume this wife had a fairly quarrelsome nature because she was originally named Sarai which means "contentious."

When the word spoken by God continued to lead this Shemite and wife, it changed both their names. She became Sarah, which means "princess." He became Abraham, which means "father of a multitude." I have a feeling that Sarah, even though she was called Princess, had a little difficulty calling Abram (which refers to heights) by his new name Father of a Multitude, since they were both getting on in years and had no children at all, much less a multitude. The positives of God's optimism frequently disturb the negatives of our nearer-sighted views.

This word of direction from God also brought into being another word, a word of promise beyond belief. The word *Mashiah* means "anointed." That word made all the travels of Abraham and Sarah meaningful. And that word was the cough drop that cleared the throats of prophets and prophetesses, judges and judgesses, poets and poetesses from Abraham to Malachi. And they all had many words to say. The hills, the desert, and the well-swept caves containing earthen jars of words scrawled on wrinkling parchment were all filled with the sounds of prophecy. Feed your hungry soul on those words; they make sense out of nonsense and songs out of despair. Turn a deaf ear to the hopeless jargon of modern wordings and fill the ears of your heart with the songs of David the king; the promises of Jeremiah who, although he wept deeply, challenged the future with words of hope; the certainty of Amos the fruit merchant; and Habakkuk of whom we know nothing but his words. Throughout all these words and songs and warnings, one word, "Mashiah," held as ballast for the boat and a poster of a sure and shining shore. And then there was silence. The silence of prophets, for none spoke. The silence of teachers, for none taught. The silence of God, who spoke not a word for four hundred years. Silence.

But in that silence God was still God and in action.

In that four hundred years, life went on. Those who had depended on the words of the prophets studied them carefully, for there was no newer news to interrupt the study. The resolute believers looked back to what God had said when he was talking. The priests held to the discipline of worship that God had spoken unto them. The law that Moses had scrawled on tablets of stone was still in place although there were those who wanted it taken out of the perimeters of the courthouse and also thought it needed a few human additions. (Several hundred of those additions made it difficult for the students of the prophets who had thought the Top Ten from Moses covered everything fairly well.) And in that four hundred years of silence, there was a new translation of that divinely guarded Old Testament. Released from its limiting language unto the Greek of the Septuagint, it now spoke in the common wordings of the day. And that one word from God that had directed Abraham, now gained pronouncement. "Mashiah" became *Messiah.* The hope of Israel. The hope of the world.

And still there was silence.

How long? How long? That must have been the question of the day. How long would the hands of a holy God cover his people's ears with the crushing fingers of his silence? Silence. Four hundred years of silence.

And then one small sound.

In the little town of Bethlehem, from a barn, a shed, a stall behind an inn came a sound from God. A baby's cry broke the stillness of that silent night. I wonder if that carpenter and his wife tried to muffle the baby's cries. The parents of Moses, generations before, had had the same problem. In fact, the world has tried to muffle that baby's cry for almost two thousand years. The voice from a makeshift manger cannot be silenced because that is the voice of God.

The child in the carpenter's shop, the young man standing on the shore, the man driving out the money changers, the man healing the leper, the man teaching from a hilltop, the man from the simplest of mangers not only had a voice; he was the voice. Messiah had come, and those who rejoiced were of his kingdom.

Isaiah had announced the Messiah's coming and his death. More than a thousand years before, this prophet Isaiah had joined the chorus of prophecy and told in grim detail of death of the innocent for the sins of the guilty. The picture had been painted by God's anointed artists of his Word, and it was all there, spread out in such clear display that any child could see it. The cleansing of the temple, the raising of the dead, the healing of the centurion's son, the feeding of the multitude, the giving of sight to the blind, the stilling of the storm at sea—the miracles that were the official card of the Messiah, the testimony of prophecy realized. And the death was part of the testimony. The picture of sacrifice, a snapshot from the garden of Eden, posted and published through the words of Moses and Jeremiah and Isaiah, and illustrated by the temple and its priests, with the sounds of the earth quaking accompanying each posing.

He died on a cross, and within the weeping and the moaning and the screams of remorse, there began an awesome silence.

The silence of God who turned his back on his only Son that he might open his arms to us. The silence of God who had said it all.

Shadowed stillness. Nothing to do but wrap the grave clothes, dare to carry the bloody body through the streets of Jerusalem. And that was daring indeed, for the Jew by law could not touch the dead body. But someone in the silence obeyed God rather than man. Was that Nicodemus? Was it Joseph of Arimathea? Was it the once rich young man who reconsidered? Was it Rufus who had helped the carrying of the cross? It was someone who dared the law in the truth of grace.

And there was silence except for the sound of a veil, a heavy tapestry, being torn from top to bottom. That planted barrier between the presence of God and his people literally torn down. And later in the silence, another sound amid the guards, the cracking of a closed grave sealed with the signature of Roman authority, yawning like a giant waking from sleep. And in the silence God spoke again.

Never underestimate the silence of God. It is his chosen punctuation, and his timing is perfect. We live in a noisy world. Sometimes God has to be silent to get us to hear him at all.

There are times when silence is healing after the suffering of loss. Sometimes silence is in itself a virtue when words would cause damage. There are times, and the most talkative ones of us must learn this, there are times when silence carries sweeter messages than spoken words.

My husband and I lived for many years in an eighth-floor apartment. Throughout our marriage we lived busy lives, happily committed to the sturdiness of our relationship. He was not a talkative man, but by the perfection of God's planning, my husband was a good listener. He not only encouraged but also equipped my work. He praised me in public and in private. But he was not a man of many words. He was a man of business. He loved his work and was committed to it fully.

Our mornings had brisk schedules. He got up early with immediate wide-awake attention. While he was dressing for the day, I—not so wide awake—would dress, fix breakfast and his lunch, make up the bed, and join him at the breakfast table. I had not known there was such a thing as breakfast before I married but soon learned that not only was there always breakfast but always the same breakfast. Breakfast was my husband's favorite meal, and he liked it without surprises. He also liked it without much conversation. Beside his place at the table was a small wireless from which was heard the ongoing conversation from workers in the field. After the blessing we ate in companionable silence—I frequently studying a script for my day of work and Lorraine listening to the morning details of his. As far as enlightening conversation, our breakfasts were silent. However, when I returned to the bedroom, I had regular messages on our eighth-floor window. Lorraine, carefully selecting the moments

I was not there, would write on the moisture collected on the window. Except for changes in the weather that foreclosed such communication, I would read scrawled greetings: "Good morning, Jeannette, I love you." Almost every morning, as he was leaving, I would tell him that some giant was obviously stalking me, proclaiming undying love. He would say in a businesslike tone, "I'll look into that!" Morning by morning in the silence, I would see a message of love. It did not last long on the window, but it will last a lifetime in my heart.

When God is silent in your life, know he is still speaking volumes. Know his silence is carefully chosen. Know there are productive actions you can take in the silence: be ready to help others in the silence; rest comfortably in the silence; get to know him better in the silence; respect the silence; but most importantly, read the words of God, carefully written inside the windows of your life to be heard in the silence: God loves you.

Dear God,

Never let me lose it, never let me forget it, never let the sophisticated advancement of so-called maturity erase its imprint, never allow the lightning of pain, the thundering of sorrow, or the crackling of disappointment drown out the sounds of its truth. Oh God, my mind is a wanderer, and like thistle bushes in a windstorm, it gets attached to things and subjects and matters that don't matter but were catchalls in the stream of modern whims and winds and wastebaskets. Keep my ears attuned to it, forbid the erasure of it, disallow its shelving on some back corner of my awareness. Keep me posted to its message because I need it fresh every morning, in sunshine and in rain, in discovery and in redundancy, in days without hours and hours that have lost their days, in the flush of fellowship or in the fallow ground of loneliness. Never let me forget it. Wind the threading of your being around my finger to remind me, fresh every morning and dominant in the night. See to it that this Holy It stays ready to clear the clinging cobwebs of doubt. Never let me forget IT this Holy IT:

> Jesus loves me! this I know,
> For the Bible tells me so;
> Little ones to Him belong;
> They are weak (Oh God, how very weak)
> But He (Oh God of my deliverance, God of my
>   life) is strong.
> Jesus loves me! this I know,
> For the Bible tells me so.

Amen.